REASON
IN SOCIETY

REASON IN SOCIETY

Volume Two of "The Life of Reason"

GEORGE SANTAYANA

ἡ γὰρ νοῦ ἐνέργεια ζωή

DOVER PUBLICATIONS, INC.
NEW YORK

Published in Canada by General Publishing Company, Ltd., 30 Lesmill Road, Don Mills, Toronto, Ontario.

Published in the United Kingdom by Constable and Company, Ltd., 10 Orange Street, London WC2H 7EG.

This Dover edition, first published in 1980, is an unabridged republication of volume two of *The Life of Reason; or the Phases of Human Progress*, originally published by Charles Scribner's Sons in 1905.

International Standard Book Number: 0-486-24003-7
Library of Congress Catalog Card Number: 80-65531

Manufactured in the United States of America
Dover Publications, Inc.
180 Varick Street
New York, N.Y. 10014

CONTENTS

BOOK II.—REASON IN SOCIETY

CHAPTER I

LOVE

Fluid existences have none but ideal goals.—Nutrition and reproduction.—Priority of the latter.—Love celebrates the initial triumph of form and is deeply ideal.—Difficulty in describing love.—One-sided or inverted theories about it.—Sexual functions its basis.—Structure the ground of faculty and faculty of duty.—Glory of animal love.—Its degradation when instincts become numerous and competitive.—Moral censure provoked.—The heart alienated from the world.—Childish ideals.—Their light all focussed on the object of love.—Three environments for love.—Subjectivity of the passion.—Machinery regulating choice.—The choice unstable.—Instinctive essence of love.—Its ideality.—Its universal scope.—Its euthanasia . . . . Pages 3–34

CHAPTER II

THE FAMILY

The family arises spontaneously.—It harmonises natural interests.—Capacity to be educated goes with immaturity at birth.—The naturally dull achieve intelligence.—It is more blessed to save than to create.—Parental instinct regards childhood only.—Handing on the torch of life.—Adventitious functions assumed by the family.—Inertia in human nature.—Family tyrannies.—Difficulty in abstracting from the family.—Possibility of substitutes.—Plato's heroic communism.—Opposite modern tendencies.—Individualism in a sense rational.—The family tamed. — Possible readjustments and reversions. — The ideal includes generation.—Inner values already lodged in this function.—Outward beneficence might be secured by experiment. . . . . Pages 35–59

CHAPTER III

INDUSTRY, GOVERNMENT, AND WAR

Patriarchal economy.—Origin of the state.—Three uses of civilisation.—Its rationality contingent.—Sources of wealth.—Excess of it possible.—Irrational industry.—Its jovial and ingenious side.—Its tyranny.—An impossible remedy.—Basis of government.—How rationality accrues. —Ferocious but useful despotisms.—Occasional advantage of being conquered.—Origin of free governments.—Their democratic tendencies.—Imperial peace.—Nominal and real status of armies.—Their action irresponsible.—Pugnacity human.—Barrack-room philosophy.—Military virtues.—They are splendid vices.—Absolute value in strife. —Sport a civilised way of preserving it.—Who shall found the universal commonwealth?..............Pages 60–87

CHAPTER IV

THE ARISTOCRATIC IDEAL

Eminence, once existing, grows by its own operation.— Its causes natural and its privileges just.—Advantage of inequality.—Fable of the belly and the members.—Fallacy in it.—Theism expresses better the aristocratic ideal.—A heaven with many mansions.—If God is defined as the human ideal, apotheosis the only paradise.—When natures differ perfections differ too.—Theory that stations actually correspond to faculty.—Its falsity.—Feeble individuality the rule.—Sophistical envy.—Inequality is not a grievance; suffering is.—Mutilation by crowding.—A hint to optimists.—How aristocracies might do good.—Man adds wrong to nature's injury.—Conditions of a just inequality ....Pages 88–113

CHAPTER V

DEMOCRACY

Democracy as an end and as a means.—Natural democracy leads to monarchy.—Artificial democracy is an extension of privilege.—Ideals and expedients.—Well-founded distrust of rulers. Yet experts, if rational, would serve common interests.—People jealous of eminence.—It is representative, but subject to decay.—Ancient citizenship a privilege.—Modern democracy industrial.—Dangers to current civilisation.—Is current civilisation a good?—Horrors of materialistic democracy.—Timocracy or socialistic aristocracy.—The difficulty the same as in all Socialism.—The masses would have to be plebeian in position and patrician in feeling.—Organisation for ideal ends breeds fanaticism.—Public spirit the life of democracy.

Pages 114–136

CHAPTER VI

FREE SOCIETY

Primacy of nature over spirit.—All experience at bottom liberal.—Social experience has its ideality too.—The self an ideal.—Romantic egotism.—Vanity.—Ambiguities of fame.—Its possible ideality.—Comradeship.—External conditions of friendship.—Identity in sex required, and in age.—Constituents of friendship.—Personal liking.—The refracting human medium for ideas.—Affection based on the refraction.—The medium must also be transparent.—Common interests indispensable.—Friendship between man and wife.—Between master and disciple.—Conflict between ideal and natural allegiance.—Automatic idealisation of heroes.............Pages 137–159

CHAPTER VII

PATRIOTISM

The creative social environment, since it eludes sense, must be represented symbolically.—Ambiguous limits of a native country, geographical and moral.—Sentimental and political patriotism.—The earth and the race the first objects of rational loyalty.—Race, when distinct, the greatest of distinctions.—"Pure" races may be morally sterile.—True nationality direction on a definite ideal.—Country well represented by domestic and civic religion.—Misleading identification of country with government.—Sporting or belligerent patriotism.—Exclusive patriotism rational only when the government supported is universally beneficent.—Accidents of birth and training affect the ideal.—They are conditions and may contribute something.—They are not ends.—The symbol for country may be a man and may become an idol.—Feudal representa-

tion sensitive but partial.—Monarchical representation
comprehensive but treacherous.—Impersonal symbols no
advantage.—Patriotism not self-interest, save to the social
man whose aims are ideal...............Pages 160–183

CHAPTER VIII

IDEAL SOCIETY

The gregarious instinct all social instincts in suspense.
—It gives rise to conscience or sympathy with the public voice.—Guises of public opinion.—Oracles and revelations.—The ideal a measure for all existences and no
existence itself.—Contrast between natural and intellectual bonds.—Appeal from man to God, from real to ideal
society.—Significant symbols revert to the concrete.—
Nature a symbol for destiny.—Representative notions
have also inherent values.—Religion and science indirectly
cognitive and directly ideal.—Their opposite outlook.—
In translating existence into human terms they give human nature its highest exercise.—Science should be mathematical and religion anthropomorphic.—Summary of this
book....................................Pages 184–205

REASON
IN SOCIETY

CHAPTER I

LOVE

**Fluid exist-
ences have
none but
ideal goals.**
 If man were a static or intelligible being, such as angels are thought to be, his life would have a single guiding interest, under which all other interests would be subsumed. His acts would explain themselves without looking beyond his given essence, and his soul would be like a musical composition, which once written out cannot grow different and once rendered can ask for nothing but, at most, to be rendered over again. In truth, however, man is an animal, a portion of the natural flux; and the consequence is that his nature has a moving centre, his functions an external reference, and his ideal a true ideality. What he strives to preserve, in preserving himself, is something which he never has been at any particular moment. He maintains his equilibrium by motion. His goal is in a sense beyond him, since it is not his experience, but a form which all experience ought to receive. The inmost texture of his being is propulsive, and there is nothing more intimately bound up with his success than mobility and devotion to transcendent aims. If

3

there is a transitive function in knowledge and an unselfish purpose in love, that is only because, at bottom, there is a self-reproductive, flying essence in all existence.

If the equilibrium of man's being were stable he would need neither nutrition, reproduction, nor sense. As it is, sense must renew his ideas and guide his instincts otherwise than as their inner evolution would demand; and regenerative processes must strive to repair beneath the constant irreparable lapse of his substance. His business is to create and remodel those organisms in which ideals are bred. In order to have a soul to save he must perpetually form it anew; he must, so to speak, *earn his own living.* In this vital labour, we may ask, is nutrition or reproduction the deeper function? Or, to put the corresponding moral question, is the body or the state the primary good?

Nutrition and reproduction.   If we view the situation from the individual's side, as self-consciousness might view it, we may reply that nutrition is fundamental, for if the body were not nourished every faculty would decay. Could nutrition only succeed and keep the body young, reproduction would be unnecessary, with its poor pretence at maintaining the mobile human form in a series of examples. On the other hand, if we view the matter from above, as science and philosophy should, we may say that nutrition is but germination of a pervasive sort, that the body is a taber-

nacle in which the transmissible human spirit
is carried for a while, a shell for the immortal
seed that dwells in it and has created it. This
seed, however, for rational estimation, is merely
a means to the existence and happiness of individuals. Transpersonal and continuous in its own
fluid being, the potential grows personal in its
ideal fulfilments. In other words, this potentiality is material (though called sometimes an idea)
and has its only value in the particular creatures
it may produce.

Priority of the
latter.
Reproduction is accordingly primary and more completely instru-
mental than nutrition is, since it serves a soul
as yet non-existent, while nutrition is useful to
a soul that already has some actuality. Reproduction initiates life and remains at life's core, a function without which no other, in the end, would
be possible. It is more central, crucial, and
representative than nutrition, which is in a way
peripheral only; it is a more typical and rudimentary act, marking the ideal's first victory over
the universal flux, before any higher function
than reproduction itself has accrued to the animal. To nourish an existing being is to presup-
pose a pause in generation; the nucleus, before
it dissolves into other individuals, gathers about
itself, for its own glory, certain temporal and
personal faculties. It lives for itself; while in
procreation it signs its own death-warrant, makes
its will, and institutes its heir.

Love cele-
brates the ini-
tial triumph of
form and is
deeply ideal.
This situation has its counterpart in feeling. Replenishment is a sort of delayed breathing, as if the animal had to hunt for air: it necessitates more activity than it contains; it engages external senses in its service and promotes intelligence. After securing a dumb satisfaction, or even in preparing it, it leaves the habits it employed free for observation and ideal exercise. Reproduction, on the contrary, depletes; it is an expense of spirit, a drag on physical and mental life; it entangles rather than liberates; it fuses the soul again into the impersonal, blind flux. Yet, since it constitutes the primary and central triumph of life, it is in itself more ideal and generous than nutrition; it fascinates the will in an absolute fashion, and the pleasures it brings are largely spiritual. For though the instrumentalities of reproduction may seem gross and trivial from a conventional point of view, its essence is really ideal, the perfect type, indeed, of ideality, since form and an identical life are therein sustained successfully by a more rhythmical flux of matter.

It may seem fanciful, even if not unmeaning, to say that a man's soul more truly survives in his son's youth than in his own decrepitude; but this principle grows more obvious as we descend to simpler beings, in which individual life is less elaborated and has not intrenched itself in so many adventitious and somewhat permanent or-

gans. In vegetables soul and seed go forth together and leave nothing but a husk behind. In
the human individual love may seem a mere incident of youth and a sentimental madness; but
that episode, if we consider the race, is indispensable to the whole drama; and if we look to
the order in which ideal interests have grown
up and to their superposition in moral experience,
love will seem the truly primitive and initiatory
passion. Consciousness, amused ordinarily by the
most superficial processes, itself bears witness to
the underlying claims of reproduction and is drawn
by it for a moment into life's central vortex; and
love, while it betrays its deep roots by the imperative force it exerts and the silence it imposes
on all current passions, betrays also its ideal mission by casting an altogether novel and poetic spell
over the mind.

Difficulty in describing love. The conscious quality of this passion differs so much in various races
and individuals, and at various points in the
same life, that no account of it will ever satisfy
everybody.* Poets and novelists never tire of

---

* The wide uses of the English word love add to the difficulty. I shall take the liberty of limiting the term here to
imaginative passion, to being in love, excluding all other
ways of loving. It follows that love—like its shadow, jealousy—will often be merely an ingredient in an actual state
of feeling; friendship and confidence, with satisfaction at
being liked in return, will often be mingled with it. We
shall have to separate physiologically things which in consciousness exist undivided, since a philosophic description is

depicting it anew; but although the experience
they tell of is fresh and unparalleled in every
individual, their rendering suffers, on the whole,
from a great monotony. Love's gesture and symp-
toms are noted and unvarying; its vocabulary
is poor and worn. Even a poet, therefore, can
give of love but a meagre expression, while the
philosopher, who renounces dramatic representation, is condemned to be avowedly inadequate.
Love, to the lover, is a noble and immense inspiration; to the naturalist it is a thin veil and
prelude to the self-assertion of lust. This opposi-
tion has prevented philosophers from doing justice to the subject. Two things need to be admitted by anyone who would not go wholly astray
in such speculation: one, that love has an animal
basis; the other, that it has an ideal object. Since
these two propositions have usually been thought
contradictory, no writer has ventured to present
more than half the truth, and that half out of its
true relations.

One-sided or inverted theories about it.   Plato, who gave eloquent expression to the ideal burden of the pas-
sion, and divined its political and cosmic message, passed over its natural history with
a few mythical fancies; and Schopenhauer, into

bound to be analytic and cannot render everything at once.
Where a poet might conceive a new composite, making it
live, a moralist must dissect the experience and rest in its
eternal elements.

whose system a naturalistic treatment would have
fitted so easily, allowed his metaphysics to carry
him at this point into verbal inanities; while, of
course, like all profane writers on the subject,
he failed to appreciate the oracles which Plato
had delivered. In popular feeling, where sentiment and observation must both make themselves
felt somehow or other, the tendency is to imagine
that love is an absolute, non-natural energy which,
for some unknown reason, or for none at all,
lights upon particular persons, and rests there
eternally, as on its ultimate goal. In other
words, it makes the origin of love divine and its
object natural: which is the exact opposite of the
truth. If it were once seen, however, that every
ideal expresses some natural function, and that
no natural function is incapable, in its free exercise, of evolving some ideal and finding justification, not in some collateral animal, but in an inherent operation like life or thought, which being
transmissible in its form is also eternal, then
the philosophy of love should not prove permanently barren. For love is a brilliant illustration
of a principle everywhere discoverable: namely,
that human reason lives by turning the friction
of material forces into the light of ideal goods.
There can be no philosophic interest in disguis-
ing the animal basis of love, or in denying its
spiritual sublimations, since all life is animal in
its origin and all spiritual in its possible fruits.

Sexual func-   Plastic matter, in transmitting its
tions its basis.   organisation, takes various courses
which it is the part of natural history to describe. Even after reproduction has become sexual, it will offer no basis for love if it does not
require a union of the two parent bodies. Did
germinal substances, unconsciously diffused, meet
by chance in the external medium and unite
there, it is obvious that whatever obsessions or
pleasures maturity might bring they would not
have the quality which men call love. But when
an individual of the opposite sex must be met
with, recognised, and pursued, and must prove
responsive, then each is haunted by the possible
other. Each feels in a generic way the presence
and attraction of his fellows; he vibrates to their
touch, he dreams of their image, he is restless
and wistful if alone. When the vague need that
solicits him is met by the presence of a possible
mate it is extraordinarily kindled. Then, if it
reaches fruition, it subsides immediately, and
after an interval, perhaps, of stupor and vital
recuperation, the animal regains his independence, his peace, and his impartial curiosity. You
might think him on the way to becoming intelligent; but the renewed nutrition and cravings of
the sexual machinery soon engross his attention
again; all his sprightly indifference vanishes before nature's categorical imperative. That fierce
and turbid pleasure, by which his obedience is
rewarded, hastens his dissolution; every day the

ensuing lassitude and emptiness give him a
clearer premonition of death. It is not figura-
tively only that his soul has passed into his offspring. The vocation to produce them was a
chief part of his being, and when that function
is sufficiently fulfilled he is superfluous in the
world and becomes partly superfluous even to
himself. The confines of his dream are narrowed.
He moves apathetically and dies forlorn.

Some echo of the vital rhythm which pervades
not merely the generations of animals, but the
seasons and the stars, emerges sometimes in consciousness; on reaching the tropics in the mortal
ecliptic, which the human individual may touch
many times without much change in his outer
fortunes, the soul may occasionally divine that it
is passing through a supreme crisis. Passion,
when vehement, may bring atavistic sentiments.
When love is absolute it feels a profound impulse
to welcome death, and even, by a transcendental
confusion, to invoke the end of the universe.*
The human soul reverts at such a moment to
what an ephemeral insect might feel, buzzing till
it finds its mate in the noon. Its whole destiny

* One example, among a thousand, is the cry of Siegfried
and Brünhilde in Wagner:

> Lachend lass' uns verderben
> Lachend zu Grunde geh'n.
> Fahr hin, Walhall's
> Leuchtende Welt! . . .
> Leb' wohl, pragende
> Götter Pracht!
> Ende in Wonne,
> Du ewig Geschlecht!

was wooing, and, that mission accomplished, it
sings its *Nunc dimittis*, renouncing heartily all
irrelevant things, now that the one fated and all-
satisfying good has been achieved. Where parental instincts exist also, nature soon shifts her
loom: a milder impulse succeeds, and a satisfaction of a gentler sort follows in the birth of children. The transcendental illusion is here cor-
rected, and it is seen that the extinction the
lovers had accepted needed not to be complete.
The death they welcomed was not without its
little resurrection. The feeble worm they had
generated bore their immortality within it.

The varieties of sexual economy are many and
to each may correspond, for all we know, a special sentiment. Sometimes the union established
is intermittent; sometimes it crowns the end of
life and dissolves it altogether; sometimes it
remains, while it lasts, monogamous; sometimes
the sexual and social alertness is constant in the
male, only periodic in the female. Sometimes
the group established for procreation endures
throughout the seasons, and from year to year;
sometimes the males herd together, as if normally they preferred their own society, until the
time of rut comes, when war arises between them
for the possession of what they have just discovered to be the fair.

Structure the ground of faculty and faculty of duty. A naturalist not ashamed to indulge his poetic imagination might
easily paint for us the drama of these

diverse loves. It suffices for our purpose to observe that the varying passions and duties which life can contain depend upon the organic functions of the animal. A fish incapable of coition, absolved from all care for its young, which it never sees or never distinguishes from the casual swimmers darting across its path, such a fish, being without social faculties or calls to cooperation, cannot have the instincts, perceptions, or emotions which belong to social beings. A male of some higher species that feels only once a year the sudden solicitations of love cannot be sentimental in all the four seasons: his headlong passion, exhausted upon its present object and dismissed at once without remainder, leaves his senses perfectly free and colourless to scrutinise his residual world. Whatever further fears or desires may haunt him will have nothing mystical or sentimental about them. He will be a man of business all the year round, and a lover only on May-day. A female that does not suffice for the rearing of her young will expect and normally receive her mate's aid long after the pleasures of love are forgotten by him. Disinterested fidelity on his part will then be her right and his duty. But a female that, once pregnant, needs, like the hen, no further co-operation on the male's part will turn from him at once with absolute indifference to brood perpetually on her eggs, undisturbed by the least sense of solitude or jealousy. And the chicks that at first follow her and find shelter under her wings will soon be forgotten also and relegated to the mechanical landscape. There is no pain in the timely snapping of the dearest bonds where society has not become a permanent organism, and perpetual friendship is not one of its possible modes.

Transcendent and ideal passions may well judge themselves to have an incomparable dignity. Yet that dignity is hardly more than what every passion, were it articulate, would assign to itself and to its objects. The dumbness of a passion may accordingly, from one point of view, be called the index of its baseness; for if it cannot ally itself with ideas its affinities can hardly lie in the rational mind nor its advocates be among the poets. But if we listen to the master-passion itself rather than to the loquacious arts it may have enlisted in its service, we shall understand that it is not self-condemned because it is silent, nor an anomaly in nature because inharmonious with human life. The fish's heartlessness is his virtue; the male bee's lasciviousness is his vocation; and if these functions were retrenched or encumbered in order to assimilate them to human excellence they would be merely dislocated. We should not produce virtue where there was vice, but defeat a possible arrangement which would have had its own vitality and order.

Glory of animal love.   Animal love is a marvellous force; and while it issues in acts that may

be followed by a revulsion of feeling, it yet
deserves a more sympathetic treatment than art
and morals have known how to accord it. Erotic
poets, to hide their want of ability to make the
dumb passion speak, have played feebly with veiled
insinuations and comic effects; while more serious sonneteers have harped exclusively on secondary and somewhat literary emotions, abstractly
conjugating the verb to love. Lucretius, in spite
of his didactic turns, has been on this subject,
too, the most ingenuous and magnificent of poets,
although he chose to confine his description to
the external history of sexual desire. It is a pity
that he did not turn, with his sublime sincerity,
to the inner side of it also, and write the drama
of the awakened senses, the poignant suasion of
beauty, when it clouds the brain, and makes the
conventional earth, seen through that bright haze,
seem a sorry fable. Western poets should not
have despised what the Orientals, in their fugitive
stanzas, seem often to have sung most exquisitely:
the joy of gazing on the beloved, of following
or being followed, of tacit understandings and
avowals, of flight together into some solitude to
people it with those ineffable confidences which
so naturally follow the outward proofs of love.
All this makes the brightest page of many a life,
the only bright page in the thin biography of
many a human animal; while if the beasts could
speak they would give us, no doubt, endless ver-

sions of the only joy in which, as we may fancy, the blood of the universe flows consciously through their hearts.

The darkness which conventionally covers this passion is one of the saddest consequences of Adam's fall. It was a terrible misfortune in man's development that he should not have been able to acquire the higher functions without deranging the lower. Why should the depths of his being be thus polluted and the most delightful of nature's mysteries be an occasion not for communion with her, as it should have remained, but for depravity and sorrow?

Its degradation when instincts become numerous and competitive. This question, asked in moral perplexity, admits of a scientific answer. Man, in becoming more complex, becomes less stably organised. His sexual instinct, instead of being intermittent, but violent and boldly declared, becomes practically constant, but is entangled in many cross-currents of desire, in many other equally imperfect adaptations of structure to various ends. Indulgence in any impulse can then easily become excessive and thwart the rest; for it may be aroused artificially and maintained from without, so that in turn it disturbs its neighbours. Sometimes the sexual instinct may be stimulated out of season by example, by a too wakeful fancy, by language, by pride—for all these forces are now working in the same field and intermingling their suggestions. At the same time the same instinct may

derange others, and make them fail at their
proper and pressing occasions.

**Moral censure
provoked.**   In consequence of such derange-
ments, reflection and public opinion
will come to condemn what in itself was perfectly innocent. The corruption of a given instinct by others and of others by it, becomes the
ground for long attempts to suppress or enslave
it. With the haste and formalism natural to language and to law, external and arbitrary limits
are set to its operation. As no inward adjustment can possibly correspond to these conventional barriers and compartments of life, a war
between nature and morality breaks out both in
society and in each particular bosom—a war in
which every victory is a sorrow and every defeat a dishonour. As one instinct after another
becomes furious or disorganised, cowardly or criminal, under these artificial restrictions, the public and private conscience turns against it all its
forces, necessarily without much nice discrimination; the frank passions of youth are met with
a grimace of horror on all sides, with *rumores
senum severiorum,* with an insistence on reticence
and hypocrisy. Such suppression is favourable
to corruption: the fancy with a sort of idiotic
ingenuity comes to supply the place of experience; and nature is rendered vicious and overlaid
with pruriency, artifice, and the love of novelty.
Hereupon the authorities that rule in such matters naturally redouble their vigilance and exag-

gerate their reasonable censure: chastity begins
to seem essentially holy and perpetual virginity
ends by becoming an absolute ideal. Thus the
disorder in man's life and disposition, when grown
intolerable, leads him to condemn the very elements out of which order might have been constituted, and to mistake his total confusion for his
total depravity.

The heart alienated from the world.   Banished from the open day, covered with mockery, and publicly ig-
nored, this necessary pleasure flour-
ishes none the less in dark places and in the
secret soul. Its familiar presence there, its intimate habitation in what is most oneself, helps
to cut the world in two and to separate the inner
from the outer life. In that mysticism which
cannot disguise its erotic affinities this disrup-
tion reaches an absolute and theoretic form; but
in many a youth little suspected of mysticism
it produces estrangement from the conventional
moralising world, which he instinctively regards
as artificial and alien. It prepares him for ex-
cursions into a private fairy-land in which un-
thought-of joys will blossom amid friendlier
magic forces. The truly good then seems to be
the fantastic, the sensuous, the prodigally unreal.
He gladly forgets the dreary world he lives in
to listen for a thousand and one nights to his
dreams.

Childish ideals.   This is the region where those who
have no conception of the Life of

Reason place the ideal; and an ideal is indeed
there but the ideal of a single and inordinate impulse. A rational mind, on the contrary, moves
by preference in the real world, cultivating all
human interests in due proportion. The love-
sick and luxurious dream-land dear to irrational
poets is a distorted image of the ideal world; but
this distortion has still an ideal motive, since it
is made to satisfy the cravings of a forgotten part
of the soul and to make a home for those elements in human nature which have been denied
overt existence. If the ideal is meantime so
sadly caricatured, the fault lies with the circumstances of life that have not allowed the sane
will adequate exercise. Lack of strength and of
opportunity makes it impossible for man to preserve all his interests in a just harmony; and his
conscious ideal, springing up as it too often does
in protest against suffering and tyranny, has not
scope and range enough to include the actual
opportunities for action. Nature herself, by
making a slave of the body, has thus made a
tyrant of the soul.

Fairy-land and a mystical heaven contain many
other factors besides that furnished by unsatisfied and objectless love. All sensuous and verbal
images may breed after their own kind in an empty brain; but these fantasies are often supported
and directed by sexual longings and vaguely luxurious thoughts. An Oriental Paradise, with its
delicate but mindless æstheticism, is above every-

thing a garden for love. To brood on such an Elysium is a likely prelude and fertile prepa-

Their light all focussed on the object of love.

ration for romantic passion. When the passion takes form it calls fancy back from its loose reveries and fixes it upon a single object. Then the ideal seems at last to have been brought down to earth. Its embodiment has been discovered amongst the children of men. Imagination narrows her range. Instead of all sorts of flatteries to sense and improbable delicious adventures, the lover imagines but a single joy: to be master of his love in body and soul. Jealousy pursues him. Even if he dreads no physical betrayal, he suffers from terror and morbid sensitiveness at every hint of mental estrangement.

This attachment is often the more absorbing the more unaccountable it seems; and as in hypnotism the subject is dead to all influences but that of the operator, so in love the heart surrenders itself entirely to the one being that has known how to touch it. That being is not selected; it is recognised and obeyed. Pre-arranged reactions in the system respond to whatever stimulus, at a propitious moment, happens to break through and arouse them pervasively. Nature has opened various avenues to that passion in whose successful operation she has so much at stake. Sometimes the magic influence asserts itself suddenly, sometimes gently and unawares. One approach, which in poetry has usurped more

than its share of attention, is through beauty;
another, less glorious, but often more efficacious,
Three environ- through surprised sense and premoni-
ments for love. tions of pleasure; a third through social sympathy and moral affinities. Contemplation, sense, and association are none of them
the essence nor even the seed of love; but any
of them may be its soil and supply it with a
propitious background. It would be mere sophistry to pretend, for instance, that love is or
should be nothing but a moral bond, the sympathy of two kindred spirits or the union of two
lives. For such an effect no passion would be
needed, as none is needed to perceive beauty or to
feel pleasure.

What Aristotle calls friendships of utility, pleasure, or virtue, all resting on common interests
of some impersonal sort, are far from possessing the quality of love, its thrill, flutter, and
absolute sway over happiness and misery. But
it may well fall to such influences to awaken or
feed the passion where it actually arises. Whatever circumstances pave the way, love does not
itself appear until a sexual affinity is declared.
When a woman, for instance, contemplating marriage, asks herself whether she really loves her
suitor or merely accepts him, the test is the possibility of awakening a sexual affinity. For this
reason women of the world often love their hus-
bands more truly than they did their lovers, because marriage has evoked an elementary feeling

which before lay smothered under a heap of coquet-
ries, vanities, and conventions.

Subjectivity of   Man, on the contrary, is polyga-
the passion.   mous by instinct, although often kept
faithful by habit no less than by duty. If his
fancy is left free, it is apt to wander. We observe this in romantic passion no less than in a
life of mere gallantry and pleasure. Sentimental
illusions may become a habit, and the shorter the
dream is the more often it is repeated, so that
any susceptible poet may find that he, like Alfred
de Musset, " must love incessantly, who once has
loved." Love is indeed much less exacting than
it thinks itself. Nine-tenths of its cause are in
the lover, for one-tenth that may be in the object.
Were the latter not accidentally at hand, an
almost identical passion would probably have been
felt for someone else; for although with acquaintance the quality of an attachment naturally adapts
itself to the person loved, and makes that person its standard and ideal, the first assault and
mysterious glow of the passion is much the same
for every object. What really affects the character of love is the lover's temperament, age, and
experience. The objects that appeal to each man
reveal his nature; but those unparalleled virtues
and that unique divinity which the lover discovers
there are reflections of his own adoration, things
that ecstasy is very cunning in. He loves what he
imagines and worships what he creates.

Those who do not consider these matters so

curiously may feel that to refer love in this way
chiefly to inner processes is at once ignominious
and fantastic. But nothing could be
more natural; the soul accurately renders, in this experience, what is going
on in the body and in the race. Nature had a
problem to solve in sexual reproduction which
would have daunted a less ruthless experimenter.
She had to bring together automatically, and at
the dictation, as they felt, of their irresponsible
wills, just the creatures that by uniting might re-
produce the species. The complete sexual reaction had to be woven together out of many incom-
plete reactions to various stimuli, reactions not
specifically sexual. The outer senses had to be
engaged, and many secondary characters found in
bodies had to be used to attract attention, until
the deeper instinctive response should have time
to gather itself together and assert itself openly.
Many mechanical preformations and reflexes must
conspire to constitute a determinate instinct. We
name this instinct after its ultimate function,
looking forward to the uses we observe it to have;
and it seems to us in consequence an inexplicable
anomaly that many a time the instinct is set in
motion when its alleged purpose cannot be fulfilled; as when love appears prematurely or too
late, or fixes upon a creature of the wrong age
or sex. These anomalies show us how nature is
built up and, far from being inexplicable, are
hints that tend to make everything clear, when

*Machinery
regulating
choice.*

once a verbal and mythical philosophy has been abandoned.

Responses which we may call sexual in view of results to which they may ultimately lead are thus often quite independent, and exist before they are drawn into the vortex of a complete and actually generative act. External stimulus and present idea will consequently be altogether inadequate to explain the profound upheaval which may ensue, if, as we say, we actually fall in love. That the senses should be played upon is nothing, if no deeper reaction is aroused. All depends on the juncture at which, so to speak, the sexual circuit is completed and the emotional currents begin to circulate. Whatever object, at such a critical moment, fills the field of consciousness becomes a signal and associate for the whole sexual mood. It is breathlessly devoured in that pause and concentration of attention, that re-arrangement of the soul, which love is conceived in; and the whole new life which that image is engulfed in is foolishly supposed to be its effect. For the image is in consciousness, but not the profound predispositions which gave it place and power.

The choice unstable. This association between passion and its signals may be merely momentary, or it may be perpetual: a Don Juan and a Dante are both genuine lovers. In a gay society the gallant addresses every woman as if she charmed him, and perhaps actually finds any kind of beauty, or mere femininity anywhere, a sufficient spur to his desire. These momentary fascinations are not necessarily false: they may for an instant be quite absorbing and irresistible; they may genuinely suffuse the whole mind. Such mercurial fire will indeed require a certain imaginative temperament; and there are many persons who, short of a life-long domestic attachment, can conceive of nothing but sordid vice. But even an inconstant flame may burn brightly, if the soul is naturally combustible. Indeed these sparks and glints of passion, just because they come and vary so quickly, offer admirable illustrations of it, in which it may be viewed, so to speak, under the microscope and in its formative stage.

Thus Plato did not hesitate to make the love of all wines, under whatever guise, excuse, or occasion, the test of a true taste for wine and an unfeigned adoration of Bacchus; and, like Lucretius after him, he wittily compiled a list of names, by which the lover will flatter the most opposite qualities, if they only succeed in arousing his inclination. To be omnivorous is one pole of true love: to be exclusive is the other. A man whose heart, if I may say so, lies deeper, hidden under a thicker coat of mail, will have less play of fancy, and will be far from finding every charm charming, or every sort of beauty a stimulus to love. Yet he may not be less prone to the tender passion, and when once smitten may be so penetrated by an unimagined tenderness and joy, that he will declare himself incapable of ever loving again, and may actually be so. Having no rivals and a deeper soil, love can ripen better in such a constant spirit; it will not waste itself in a continual patter of little pleasures and illusions. But unless the passion of it is to die down, it must somehow assert its universality: what it loses in diversity it must gain in applicability. It must become a principle of action and an influence colouring everything that is dreamt of; otherwise it would have lost its dignity and sunk into a dead memory or a domestic bond.

Instinctive essence of love.   True love, it used to be said, is love at first sight. Manners have much to do with such incidents, and the race which happens to set, at a given time, the fashion in literature makes its temperament public and exercises a sort of contagion over all men's fancies. If women are rarely seen and ordinarily not to be spoken to; if all imagination has to build upon is a furtive glance or casual motion, people fall in love at first sight. For they must fall in love somehow, and any stimulus is enough if none more powerful is forthcoming. When society, on the contrary, allows constant and easy intercourse between the sexes, a first impression, if not reinforced, will soon be hidden and obliterated by others. Acquaintance becomes necessary for love when it is necessary for memory. But what makes true love is not the information conveyed by acquaintance, not any circumstantial charms that may be therein discovered: it is still a deep and dumb instinctive affinity, an inexplicable emotion seizing the heart, an influence organising the world, like a luminous crystal, about one magic point. So that although love seldom springs up suddenly in these days into anything like a full-blown passion, it is sight, it is presence, that makes in time a conquest over the heart; for all virtues, sympathies, confidences will fail to move a man to tenderness and to worship, unless a poignant effluence from the object envelop him, so that he begins to walk, as it were, in a dream.

Not to believe in love is a great sign of dulness. There are some people so indirect and lumbering that they think all real affection must rest on circumstantial evidence. But a finely constituted being is sensitive to its deepest affinities. This is precisely what refinement consists in, that we may feel in things immediate and infinitesimal a sure premonition of things ultimate and important. Fine senses vibrate at once to harmonies which it may take long to verify; so sight is finer than touch, and thought than sensation. Well-bred instinct meets reason half-way, and is prepared for the consonances that may follow. Beautiful things, when taste is formed, are obviously and unaccountably beautiful. The grounds we may bring ourselves to assign for our preferences are discovered by analysing those preferences, and articulate judgments follow upon emotions which they ought to express, but which they sometimes sophisticate. So, too, the reasons we give for love either express what it feels or else are insincere, attempting to justify at the bar of reason and convention something which is far more primitive than they and underlies them both. True instinct can dispense with such excuses. It appeals to the event and is justified by the response which nature makes to it. It is, of course, far from infallible; it cannot dominate circumstances, and has no discursive knowledge; but it is presumably true, and what it foreknows is always essentially possible. Unrealisable it may indeed be in the jumbled context of this world, where the Fates, like an absent-minded printer, seldom allow a single line to stand perfect and unmarred.

The profoundest affinities are those most readily felt, and though a thousand later considerations may overlay and override them, they remain a background and standard for all happiness. If we trace them out we succeed. If we put them by, although in other respects we may call ourselves happy, we inwardly know that we have dismissed the ideal, and all that was essentially possible has not been realised. Love in that case still owns a hidden and potential object, and we sanctify, perhaps, whatever kindnesses or partialities we indulge in by a secret loyalty to something impersonal and unseen. Such reserve, such religion, would not have been necessary had things responded to our first expectations. We might then have identified the ideal with the object that happened to call it forth. The Life of Reason might have been led instinctively, and we might have been guided by nature herself into the ways of peace.

Its ideality. As it is, circumstances, false steps, or the mere lapse of time, force us to shuffle our affections and take them as they come, or as we are suffered to indulge them. A mother is followed by a boyish friend, a friend by a girl, a girl by a wife, a wife by a child, a child by an idea. A divinity passes through these various temples; they may all remain standing, and we may continue our cult in them without outward change, long after the god has fled from the last into his native heaven. We may try to convince ourselves that we have lost nothing when we have lost all. We may take comfort in praising the mixed and perfunctory attachments which cling to us by force of habit and duty, repeating the empty names of creatures that have long ceased to be what we once could love, and assuring ourselves that we have remained constant, without admitting that the world, which is in irreparable flux, has from the first been betraying us.

Ashamed of being so deeply deceived, we may try to smile cynically at the glory that once shone upon us, and call it a dream. But cynicism is wasted on the ideal. There is indeed no idol ever identified with the ideal which honest experience, even without cynicism, will not some day unmask and discredit. Every real object must cease to be what it seemed, and none could ever be what the whole soul desired. Yet what the soul desires is nothing arbitrary. Life is no objectless dream, but continually embodies, with varying success, the potentialities it contains and that prompt desire. Everything that satisfies at all, even if partially and for an instant, justifies aspiration and rewards it. Existence, however, cannot be arrested; and only the transmissible forms of things can endure, to match the transmissible faculties which living beings hand down to one another. The ideal is accordingly significant, perpetual, and as constant as the nature it expresses; but it can never itself exist, nor can its particular embodiments endure.

Its universal scope.   Love is accordingly only half an illusion; the lover, but not his love, is deceived. His madness, as Plato taught, is divine; for though it be folly to identify the idol with the god, faith in the god is inwardly justified. That egregious idolatry may therefore be interpreted ideally and given a symbolic scope worthy of its natural causes and of the mystery it comes to celebrate. The lover knows much more about absolute good and universal beauty than any logician or theologian, unless the latter, too, be lovers in disguise. Logical universals are terms in discourse, without vital ideality, while tradi-

tional gods are at best natural existences, more
or less indifferent facts. What the lover comes
upon, on the contrary, is truly persuasive, and
witnesses to itself, so that he worships from the
heart and beholds what he worships. That the
true object is no natural being, but an ideal form
essentially eternal and capable of endless embodiments, is far from abolishing its worth; on the
contrary, this fact makes love ideally relevant to
generation, by which the human soul and body
may be for ever renewed, and at the same time
makes it a thing for large thoughts to be focussed
upon, a thing representing all rational aims.

Whenever this ideality is absent and a lover sees
nothing in his mistress but what everyone else
may find in her, loving her honestly in her unvar-
nished and accidental person, there is a friendly
and humorous affection, admirable in itself, but
no passion or bewitchment of love; she is a member of his group, not a spirit in his pantheon.
Such an affection may be altogether what it should
be; it may bring a happiness all the more stable
because the heart is quite whole, and no divine
shaft has pierced it. It is hard to stanch wounds
inflicted by a god. The glance of an ideal love is
terrible and glorious, foreboding death and immortality together. Love could not be called
divine without platitude if it regarded nothing
but its nominal object; to be divine it must not
envisage an accidental good but the principle of
goodness, that which gives other goods their ulti-

mate meaning, and makes all functions useful.
Love is a true natural religion; it has a visible
cult, it is kindled by natural beauties and bows
to the best symbol it may find for its hope; it
sanctifies a natural mystery; and, finally, when
understood, it recognises that what it worshipped
under a figure was truly the principle of all good.

The loftiest edifices need the deepest foundations. Love would never take so high a flight
unless it sprung from something profound and
elementary. It is accordingly most truly love
when it is irresistible and fatal. The substance
of all passion, if we could gather it together,
would be the basis of all ideals, to which all
goods would have to refer. Love actually accom-
plishes something of the sort; being primordial
it underlies other demands, and can be wholly
satisfied only by a happiness which is ultimate
and comprehensive. Lovers are vividly aware
of this fact: their ideal, apparently so inarticu-
late, seems to them to include everything. It
shares the mystical quality of all primitive life.
Sophisticated people can hardly understand how
vague experience is at bottom, and how truly that
vagueness supports whatever clearness is afterward attained. They cling to the notion that
nothing can have a spiritual scope that does not
spring from reflection. But in that case life itself,
which brings reflection about, would never support
spiritual interests, and all that is moral would be
unnatural and consequently self-destructive. In

truth, all spiritual interests are supported by
animal life; in this the generative function is
fundamental; and it is therefore no paradox, but
something altogether fitting, that if that function
realised all it comprises, nothing human would remain outside.   Such an ultimate fulfilment would
differ, of course, from a first satisfaction, just
as all that reproduction reproduces differs from
the reproductive function itself, and vastly ex-
ceeds it.   All organs and activities which are inherited, in a sense, grow out of the reproductive
process and serve to clothe it; so that when the
generative energy is awakened all that can ever
be is virtually called up and, so to speak, made
consciously potential; and love yearns for the
universe of values.

This secret is gradually revealed to
Its euthanasia. those who are inwardly attentive and
allow love to teach them something.   A man who
has truly loved, though he may come to recognise
the thousand incidental illusions into which love
may have led him, will not recant its essential
faith.   He will keep his sense for the ideal and
his power to worship.   The further objects by
which these gifts will be entertained will vary
with the situation.   A philosopher, a soldier, and
a courtesan will express the same religion in different ways.   In fortunate cases love may glide
imperceptibly into settled domestic affections, giving them henceforth a touch of ideality; for when
love dies in the odour of sanctity people venerate

his relics. In other cases allegiance to the ideal may appear more sullenly, breaking out in whims, or in little sentimental practices which might seem half-conventional. Again it may inspire a religious conversion, charitable works, or even artistic labours. In all these ways people attempt more or less seriously to lead the Life of Reason, expressing outwardly allegiance to whatever in their minds has come to stand for the ideal. If to create was love's impulse originally, to create is its effort still, after it has been chastened and has received some rational extension. The machinery which serves reproduction thus finds kindred but higher uses, as every organ does in a liberal life; and what Plato called a desire for birth in beauty may be sublimated even more, until it yearns for an ideal immortality in a transfigured world, a world made worthy of that love which its children have so often lavished on it in their dreams.

CHAPTER II

THE FAMILY

The family arises spontaneously. Love is but a prelude to life, an overture in which the theme of the impending work is exquisitely hinted at, but which remains nevertheless only a symbol and a promise. What is to follow, if all goes well, begins presently to appear. Passion settles down into possession, courtship into partnership, pleasure into habit. A child, half mystery and half plaything, comes to show us what we have done and to make its consequences perpetual. We see that by indulging our inclinations we have woven about us a net from which we cannot escape: our choices, bearing fruit, begin to manifest our destiny. That life which once seemed to spread out infinitely before us is narrowed to one mortal career. We learn that in morals the infinite is a chimera, and that in accomplishing anything definite a man renounces everything else. He sails henceforth for one point of the compass.

It harmonises natural interests. The family is one of nature's masterpieces. It would be hard to conceive a system of instincts more nicely adjusted, where the constituents should represent

35

or support one another better. The husband has an interest in protecting the wife, she in serving the husband. The weaker gains in authority and safety, the wilder and more unconcerned finds a help-mate at home to take thought for his daily necessities. Parents lend children their experience and a vicarious memory; children endow their parents with a vicarious immortality.

The long childhood in the human race has made it possible and needful to transmit acquired experience: possible, because the child's brain, being immature, allows instincts and habits to be formed after birth, under the influence of that very environment in which they are to operate; and also needful, since children are long incapable of providing for themselves and compel their parents, if the race is not to die out, to continue their care, and to diversify it. To be born half-made is an immense advantage. Structure performed is formed blindly; the *a priori* is as dangerous in life as in philosophy. Only the cruel workings of compulsion and extermination keep what is spontaneous in any creature harmonious with the world it is called upon to live in. Nothing but casual variations could permanently improve such a creature; and casual variations will seldom improve it. But if experience can co-operate in forming instincts, and if human nature can be partly a work of art, mastery can be carried

Capacity to be educated goes with immaturity at birth.

quickly to much greater lengths. This is the secret of man's pre-eminence. His liquid brain is unfit for years to control action advantageously. He has an age of play which is his apprenticeship; and he is formed unawares by a series of selective experiments, of curious gropings, while he is still under tutelage and suffers little by his mistakes.

The naturally dull achieve intelligence. Had all intelligence been developed in the womb, as it might have been, nothing essential could have been learned afterward. Mankind would have contained nothing but doctrinaires, and the arts would have stood still for ever. Capacity to learn comes with dependence on education; and as that animal which at birth is most incapable and immature is the most teachable, so too those human races which are most precocious are most incorrigible, and while they seem the cleverest at first prove ultimately the least intelligent. They depend less on circumstances, but do not respond to them so well. In some nations everybody is by nature so astute, versatile, and sympathetic that education hardly makes any difference in manners or mind; and it is there precisely that generation follows generation without essential progress, and no one ever remakes himself on a better plan. It is perhaps the duller races, with a long childhood and a brooding mind, that bear the hopes of the world within them, if only nature avails to execute what she has planned on so great a scale.

Generation answers no actual de-
It is more blessed to save than to create. mand except that existing in the parents, and it establishes a new demand
without guaranteeing its satisfaction. Birth is a
benefit only problematically and by anticipation,
on the presumption that the faculties newly embodied are to be exercised successfully. The second function of the family, to rear, is therefore
higher than the first. To foster and perfect a
life after it has been awakened, to co-operate
with a will already launched into the world, is a
positive good work. It has a moral quality and
is not mere vegetation; for in expressing the
agent and giving him ideal employment, it helps
the creature affected to employ itself better, too,
and to find expression. In propagating and sow-
ing broadcast precarious beings there is fertility
only, such as plants and animals may have; but
there is charity in furthering what is already
rooted in existence and is striving to live.

This principle is strikingly illustrated in religion. When the Jews had become spiritual they
gave the name of Father to Jehovah, who had before been only the Lord of Armies or the architect
of the cosmos. A mere source of being would not
deserve to be called father, unless it shared its
creatures' nature and therefore their interests.
A deity not so much responsible for men's existence or situation as solicitous for their welfare,
who pitied a weakness he could not have intended
and was pleased by a love he could not command,

might appropriately be called a father. It then becomes possible to conceive moral intercourse and mutual loyalty between God and man, such as Hebrew religion so earnestly insisted on; for both then have the same interests in the world and look toward the same consummations. So the natural relations subsisting between parents and children become moral when it is not merely derivation that unites them, but community of purpose. The father then represents his children while they are under his tutelage, and afterward they represent him, carrying on his arts and inheriting his mind.

These arts in some cases are little more than retarded instincts, faculties that ripen late and that manifest themselves without special instruction when the system is mature. So a bird feeds her young until they are fledged and can provide for themselves. Parental functions in such **Parental instinct regards childhood only.** cases are limited to nursing the extremely young. This phase of the instinct, being the most primitive and fundamental, is most to be relied upon even in man. Especially in the mother, care for the children's physical well-being is unfailing to the end. She understands the vegetative soul, and the first lispings of sense and sentiment in the child have an absorbing interest for her. In that region her skill and delights are miracles of nature; but her insight and keenness gradually fade as the children grow older. Seldom is the private and ideal

life of a young son or daughter a matter in which
the mother shows particular tact or for which
she has instinctive respect. Even rarer is any
genuine community in life and feeling between
parents and their adult children. Often the parent's influence comes to be felt as a dead con-
straint, the more cruel that it cannot be thrown
off without unkindness; and what makes the
parents' claim at once unjust and pathetic is that
it is founded on passionate love for a remembered
being, the child once wholly theirs, that no longer
exists in the man.

To train character and mind would seem to be
a father's natural office, but as a matter of fact
he commonly delegates that task to society. The
fledgling venturing for the first time into the air
may learn of his father and imitate his style of
flight; but once launched into the open it will
find the whole sky full of possible masters. The
one ultimately chosen will not necessarily be the
nearest; in reason it should be the most congenial,
from whom most can be learned. To choose an
imitable hero is the boy's first act of freedom;
his heart grows by finding its elective affinities,
and it grows most away from home. It will grow
also by returning there, when home has become
a part of the world or a refuge from it; but even
then the profoundest messages will come from religion and from solitary dreams. A consequence
is that parental influence, to be permanent, requires that the family should be hedged about

with high barriers and that the father be endowed with political and religious authority. He can then exercise the immense influence due to all tradition, which he represents, and all law, which he administers; but it is not his bare instincts as a father that give him this ascendency. It is a social system that has delegated to him most of its functions, so that all authority flows through him, and he retails justice and knowledge, besides holding all wealth in his hand. When the father, apart from these official prerogatives, is eager and able to mould his children's minds, a new relation half natural and half ideal, which is friendship, springs up between father and son. In this ties of blood merely furnish the opportunity, and what chiefly counts is a moral impulse, on the one side, to beget children in the spirit, and on the other a youthful hunger for experience and ideas.

Handing on the torch of life. If *Nunc dimittis* is a psalm for love to sing, it is even more appropriate for parental piety. On seeing heirs and representatives of ours already in the world, we are inclined to give them place and trust them to realise our foiled ambitions. They, we fancy, will be more fortunate than we; we shall have screened them from whatever has most maimed our own lives. Their purer souls, as we imagine, will reach better things than are now possible to ours, distracted and abused so long. We commit the blotted manuscript of our lives more willingly to the flames, when we find the immortal text already half engrossed in a fairer copy. In all this there is undoubtedly a measure of illusion, since little clear improvement is ordinarily possible in the world, and while our children may improve upon us in some respects, the devil will catch them unprepared in another quarter. Yet the hope in question is a transcript of primary impersonal functions to which nature, at certain levels, limits the animal will. To keep life going was, in the beginning, the sole triumph of life. Even when nothing but reproduction was aimed at or attained, existence was made possible and ideally stable by securing so much; and when the ideal was enlarged so as to include training and rearing the new generation, life was even better intrenched and protected. Though further material progress may not be made easier by this development, since more dangers become fatal as beings grow complex and mutually dependent, a great step in moral progress has at any rate been taken.

In itself, a desire to see a child grow and prosper is just as irrational as any other absolute desire; but since the child also desires his own happiness, the child's will sanctions and supports the father's. Thus two irrationalities, when they conspire, make one rational life. The father's instinct and sense of duty are now vindicated experimentally in the child's progress, while the son, besides the joy of living, has the pious func-

tion of satisfying his parent's hopes. Even if life
could achieve nothing more than this, it would
have reached something profoundly natural and
perfectly ideal. In patriarchal ages men feel it
is enough to have inherited their human patri-
mony, to have enjoyed it, and to hand it down
unimpaired. He who is not childless goes down
to his grave in peace. Reason may afterward
come to larger vistas and more spiritual aims,
but the principle of love and responsibility will
not be altered. It will demand that wills be made
harmonious and satisfactions compatible.

Adventitious functions assumed by the family. Life is experimental, and whatever
performs some necessary function,
and cannot be discarded, is a safe nucleus for many a parasite, a starting-
point for many new experiments. So the family,
in serving to keep the race alive, becomes a point
of departure for many institutions. It assumes
offices which might have been allotted to some
other agency, had not the family pre-empted
them, profiting by its established authority and
annexing them to its domain. In no civilised
community, for instance, has the union of man
and wife been limited to its barely necessary
period. It has continued after the family was
reared and has remained life-long; it has commonly involved a common dwelling and religion
and often common friends and property. Again,
the children's emancipation has been put off in-
definitely. The Roman father had a perpetual

jurisdiction and such absolute authority that, in the palmy days of the Roman family, no other subsisted over it. He alone was a citizen and responsible to the state, while his household were subject to him in law, as well as in property and religion. In simple rural communities the family has often been also the chief industrial unit, almost all necessaries being produced under domestic economy.

Now the instincts and delights which nature associates with reproduction cannot stretch so far. Their magic fails, and the political and industrial family, which still thinks itself natural, is in truth casual and conventional. There is no real instinct to protect those who can already protect themselves; nor have they any profit in obeying nor, in the end, any duty to do so. A *patria potestas* much prolonged or extended is therefore an abuse and prolific in abuses. The chieftain's mind, not being ruled by paternal instincts, will pursue arbitrary personal ends, and it is hardly to be expected that his own wealth or power or ideal interests will correspond with those of his subjects. The government and supervision required by adults is what we call political; it should stretch over all families alike. To annex this

Inertia in human nature. political control to fatherhood is to confess that social instinct is singularly barren, and that the common mind is not plastic enough to devise new organs appropriate to the functions which a large society involves.

After all, the family is an early expedient and in many ways irrational. If the race had developed a special sexless class to be nurses, pedagogues, and slaves, like the workers among ants and bees, and if lovers had never been tied together by a bond less ethereal than ideal passion, then the family would have been unnecessary. Such a division of labour would doubtless have involved evils of its own, but it would have obviated some drags and vexations proper to the family. For we pay a high price for our conquests in this quarter, and the sweets of home are balanced not only by its tenderer sorrows, but by a thousand artificial prejudices, enmities, and restrictions. It takes patience to appreciate domestic bliss; volatile spirits prefer unhappiness. Young men escape as soon as they can, at least in fancy, into the wide world; all prophets are homeless and all inspired artists; philosophers think out some communism or other, and monks put it in practice. There is indeed no more irrational ground for living together than that we have sprung from the same loins. They say blood is thicker than water; yet similar forces easily compete while dissimilar forces may perhaps co-operate. It is the end that is sacred, not the beginning. A common origin unites reasonable creatures only if it involves common thoughts and purposes; and these may bind together individuals of the most remote races and ages, when once they have discovered one another. It is difficulties of access, ignorance, and material confinement that shut in the heart to its narrow loyalties; and perhaps greater mobility, science, and the mingling of nations will one day reorganise the moral world. It was a pure spokesman of the spirit who said that whosoever should do the will of his *Father who was in heaven,* the same was his brother and sister and mother.

Family tyran-nies. The family also perpetuates accidental social differences, exaggerating and making them hereditary; it thus defeats that just moiety of the democratic ideal which demands that all men should have equal opportunities. In human society chance only decides what education a man shall receive, what wealth and influence he shall enjoy, even what religion and profession he shall adopt. People shudder at the system of castes which prevails in India; but is not every family a little caste? Was a man assigned to his family because he belonged to it in spirit, or can he choose another? Half the potentialities in the human race are thus stifled, half its incapacities fostered and made inveterate. The family, too, is largely responsible for the fierce prejudices that prevail about women, about religion, about seemly occupations, about war, death, and honour. In all these matters men judge in a blind way, inspired by a feminine passion that has no mercy for anything that eludes the traditional household, not even for its members' souls.

At the same time there are insuper-
able difficulties in proposing any substitute for the family. In the first
place, all society at present rests on
this institution, so that we cannot easily discern
which of our habits and sentiments are parcels
of it, and which are attached to it adventitiously
and have an independent basis. A reformer hew-
ing so near to the tree's root never knows how
much he may be felling. Possibly his own ideal
would lose its secret support if what it condemns
had wholly disappeared. For instance, it is conceivable that a communist, abolishing the family
in order to make opportunities equal and remove
the more cruel injustices of fortune, might be
drying up that milk of human kindness which
had fed his own enthusiasm; for the foundlings
which he decreed were to people the earth might
at once disown all socialism and prove a brood of
inhuman egoists. Or, as not wholly contemptible
theories have maintained, it might happen that
if fathers were relieved of care for their children
and children of all paternal suasion, human virtue
would lose its two chief stays.

Difficulty in abstracting from the family.

On the other hand, an opposite
danger is present in this sort of speculation. Things now associated with the family
may not depend upon it, but might flourish
equally well in a different soil. The family being
the earliest and closest society into which men
enter, it assumes the primary functions which

Possibility of substitutes.

all society can exercise. Possibly if any other
institution had been first in the field it might
have had a comparable moral influence. One of
the great lessons, for example, which society has
to teach its members is that society exists. The
child, like the animal, is a colossal egoist, not
from a want of sensibility, but through his deep
transcendental isolation. The mind is naturally
its own world and its solipsism needs to be broken
down by social influence. The child must learn
to sympathise intelligently, to be considerate,
rather than instinctively to love and hate: his
imagination must become cognitive and dramati-
cally just, instead of remaining, as it naturally is,
sensitively, selfishly fanciful.

To break down transcendental conceit is a function usually confided to the family, and yet the
family is not well fitted to perform it. To mothers and nurses their darlings are always exceptional; even fathers and brothers teach a child
that he is very different from other creatures and
of infinitely greater consequence, since he lies
closer to their hearts and may expect from them
all sorts of favouring services. The whole household, in proportion as it spreads about the child a
brooding and indulgent atmosphere, nurses wil-
fulness and illusion. For this reason the noblest
and happiest children are those brought up, as in
Greece or England, under simple general conventions by persons trained and hired for the
purpose. The best training in character is found

in very large families or in schools, where boys educate one another. Priceless in this regard is athletic exercise; for here the test of ability is visible, the comparison not odious, the need of co-operation clear, and the consciousness of power genuine and therefore ennobling. Socratic dialectic is not a better means of learning to know oneself. Such self-knowledge is objective and free from self-consciousness; it sees the self in a general medium and measures it by a general law.

Even the tenderer associations of home might, under other circumstances, attach to other objects. Consensus of opinion has a distorting effect, sometimes, on ideal values. A thing which almost everyone agrees in prizing, because it has played some part in every life, tends to be valued above more important elements in personal happiness that may not have been shared. So wealth, religion, military victory have more rhetorical than efficacious worth. The family might well be, to some extent, a similar idol of the tribe. Everyone has had a father and a mother; but how many have had a friend? Everyone likes to remember many a joy and even sorrow of his youth which was linked with family occasions; but to name a man's more private memories, attached to special surroundings, would awaken no response in other minds. Yet these other surroundings may have been no less stimulating to emotion, and if familiar to all might be spoken of with as much conventional effect. This appears so soon as any experience is diffused enough to enable a tradition to arise, so that the sentiment involved can find a social echo. Thus there is a loyalty, very powerful in certain quarters, toward school, college, club, regiment, church, and country. Who shall say that such associations, had they sprung up earlier and been more zealously cultivated, or were they now reinforced by more general sympathy, would not breed all the tenderness and infuse all the moral force which most men now derive from the family?

Plato's heroic communism. Nevertheless, no suggested substitute for the family is in the least satisfactory. Plato's is the best grounded in reason; but to succeed it would have to count on a degree of virtue absolutely unprecedented in man. To be sure, the Platonic regimen, if it demands heroism for its inception, provides in its scientific breeding and education a means of making heroism perpetual. But to submit to such reforming regulations men would first have to be reformed; it would not suffice, as Plato suggested, merely to enslave them and to introduce scientific institutions by despotic decrees. For in such a case there would be all manner of evasions, rebellions, and corruptions. If marriage founded on inclination and mutual consent is so often broken surreptitiously or by open divorce, what should we expect amongst persons united and separated by governmental policy? The love of home is a human instinct. Princes who marry for political reasons often find a second household necessary to their happiness, although every motive of honour, policy, religion, and patriotism makes with overwhelming force against such irregularities; and the celibate priesthood, presumably taking its vows freely and under the influence of religious zeal, often revert in practice to a sort of natural marriage. It is true that Plato's citizens were not to be celibates, and the senses would have had no just cause for rebellion; but would the heart have been satisfied? Could passion or habit submit to such regulation?

Even when every concession is made to the god-like simplicity and ardour which that Platonic race was to show, a greater difficulty appears. Apparently the guardians and auxiliaries, a small minority in the state, were alone to submit to this regimen: the rest of the people, slaves, tradesmen, and foreigners, were to live after their own devices and were, we may suppose, to retain the family. So that, after all, Plato in this matter proposes little more than what military and monastic orders have actually done among Christians: to institute a privileged unmarried class in the midst of an ordinary community. Such a proposal, therefore, does not abolish the family.

Opposite modern tendencies. Those forms of free love or facile divorce to which radical opinion and practice incline in these days tend to transform the family without abolishing it. Many unions might continue to be lasting, and the children

in any case would remain with one or the other
parent. The family has already suffered greater
transformations than that suggested by this sect.
Polygamy persists, involving its own type of morals and sentiment, and savage tribes show even
more startling conventions. Nor is it reasonable to dismiss all ideals but the Christian and
then invoke Christian patience to help us endure
the consequent evils, which are thus declared to
be normal. No evil is normal. Of course virtue
is the cure for every abuse; but the question
is the true complexion of virtue and the regimen
needful to produce it. Christianity, with its
non-political and remedial prescriptions, in the
form of prayer, penance, and patience, has left
the causes of every evil untouched. It has so
truly come to call the sinner to repentance that its
occupation would be gone if once the sin could
be abolished.

Individualism
in a sense ra-
tional.

While a desirable form of society
entirely without the family is hard to
conceive, yet the general tendency in
historic times, and the marked tendency in periods
of ripe development, has been toward individualism. Individualism is in one sense the only
possible ideal; for whatever social order may be
most valuable can be valuable only for its effect
on conscious individuals. Man is of course a
social animal and needs society first that he may
come safely into being, and then that he may
have something interesting to do. But society

itself is no animal and has neither instincts, interests, nor ideals. To talk of such things is either to speak metaphorically or to think mythically; and myths, the more currency they acquire, pass the more easily into superstitions. It would be a gross and pedantic superstition to venerate any form of society in itself, apart from the safety, breadth, or sweetness which it lent to individual happiness. If the individual may be justly subordinated to the state, not merely for the sake of a future freer generation, but permanently and in the ideal society, the reason is simply that such subordination is a part of man's natural devotion to things rational and impersonal, in the presence of which alone he can be personally happy. Society, in its future and its past, is a natural object of interest like art or science; it exists, like them, because only when lost in such rational objects can a free soul be active and immortal. But all these ideals are terms in some actual life, not alien ends, important to nobody, to which, notwithstanding, everybody is to be sacrificed.

Individualism is therefore the only ideal possible. The excellence of societies is measured by what they provide for their members. A cumbrous and sanctified social order manifests dulness, and cannot subsist without it. It immerses man in instrumentalities, weighs him down with atrophied organs, and by subjecting him eternally to fruitless sacrifices renders him stupid and superstitious and ready to be himself tyrannical when the opportunity occurs. A sure sign of having escaped barbarism is therefore to feel keenly the pragmatic values belonging to all institutions, to look deep into the human sanctions of things. Greece was on this ground more civilised than Rome, and Athens more than Sparta. Ill-governed communities may be more intelligent than well-governed ones, when people feel the motive and partial advantage underlying the abuses they tolerate (as happens where slavery or nepotism is prevalent), but when on the other hand no reason is perceived for the good laws which are established (as when law is based on revelation). The effort to adjust old institutions suddenly to felt needs may not always be prudent, because the needs most felt may not be the deepest, yet so far as it goes the effort is intelligent.

The family tamed.   The family in a barbarous age remains sacrosanct and traditional; nothing in its law, manners, or ritual is open to amendment. The unhappiness which may consequently overtake individuals is hushed up or positively blamed, with no thought of tinkering with the holy institutions which are its cause. Civilised men think more and cannot endure objectless tyrannies. It is inevitable, therefore, that as barbarism recedes the family should become more sensitive to its members' personal interests. Husband and wife, when they are happily matched, are in liberal communities more truly united than before, because such closer friendship expresses their personal inclination. Children are still cared for, because love of them is natural, but they are ruled less and sooner suffered to choose their own associations. They are more largely given in charge to persons not belonging to the family, especially fitted to supply their education. The whole, in a word, exists more and more for the sake of the parts, and the closeness, duration, and scope of family ties comes to vary greatly in different households. Barbaric custom, imposed in all cases alike without respect of persons, yields to a regimen that dares to be elastic and will take pains to be just.

Possible readjustments and reversions. How far these liberties should extend and where they would pass into license and undermine rational life, is another question. The pressure of circumstances is what ordinarily forces governments to be absolute. Political liberty is a sign of moral and economic independence. The family may safely weaken its legal and customary authority so long as the individual can support and satisfy himself. Children evidently never can; consequently they must remain in a family or in some artificial substitute for it which would be no less coercive. But to what extent men and women, in a future age, may need to rely on ties of consanguinity or marriage in order not to grow solitary, purposeless, and depraved, is for prophets only to predict. If changes continue in the present direction much that is now in bad odour may come to be accepted as normal. It might happen, for instance, as a consequence of woman's independence, that mothers alone should be their children's guardians and sole mistresses in their houses; the husband, if he were acknowledged at all, having at most a pecuniary responsibility for his offspring. Such an arrangement would make a stable home for the children, while leaving marriage dissoluble at the will of either party.

It may well be doubted, however, whether women, if given every encouragement to establish and protect themselves, would not in the end fly again into man's arms and prefer to be drudges and mistresses at home to living disciplined and submerged in some larger community. Indeed, the effect of women's emancipation might well prove to be the opposite of what was intended. Really free and equal competition between men and women might reduce the weaker sex to such graceless inferiority that, deprived of the deference and favour they now enjoy, they should find themselves entirely without influence. In that case they would have to begin again at the bottom and appeal to arts of seduction and to men's fondness in order to regain their lost social position.

The ideal includes generation.
There is a certain order in progress which it is impossible to retract. An advance must not subvert its own basis nor revoke the interest which it furthers. While hunger subsists the art of ploughing is rational; had agriculture abolished appetite it

would have destroyed its own rationality. Similarly no state of society is to be regarded as ideal in which those bodily functions are supposed to be suspended which created the ideal by suggesting their own perfect exercise. If old age and death were abolished, reproduction, indeed, would become unnecessary: its pleasures would cease to charm the mind, and its results—pregnancy, childbirth, infancy—would seem positively horrible. But so long as reproduction is necessary the ideal of life must include it. Otherwise we should be constructing not an ideal of life but some dream of non-human happiness, a dream whose only remnant of ideality would be borrowed from such actual human functions as it still expressed indirectly. The true ideal must speak for all necessary and compatible functions. Man being an inevitably reproductive animal his reproductive function must be included in his perfect life.

Inner values already lodged in this function. Now, any function to reach perfection it must fulfil two conditions: it must be delightful in itself, endowing its occasions and results with ideal interest, and it must also co-operate harmoniously with all other functions so that life may be profitable and happy. In the matter of reproduction nature has already fulfilled the first of these conditions in its essentials. It has indeed superabundantly fulfilled them, and not only has love appeared in man's soul, the type and symbol of all vital perfection, but a tenderness and

charm, a pathos passing into the frankest joy, has
been spread over pregnancy, birth, and childhood.
If many pangs and tears still prove how tentative
and violent, even here, are nature's most brilliant
feats, science and kindness may strive not unsuc-
cessfully to diminish or abolish those profound
traces of evil. But reproduction will not be perfectly organised until the second condition is
fulfilled as well, and here nature has as yet been
more remiss. Family life, as Western nations
possess it, is still regulated in a very bungling,
painful, and unstable manner. Hence, in the
first rank of evils, prostitution, adultery, divorce,
improvident and unhappy marriages; and in the
second rank, a morality compacted of three inharmonious parts, with incompatible ideals, each in
its way legitimate: I mean the ideals of passion,
of convention, and of reason; add, besides, genius
and religion thwarted by family ties, single lives
empty, wedded lives constrained, a shallow gallantry, and a dull virtue.

Outward be-   How to surround the natural sancti-
neficence   ties of wedlock with wise custom and
might be se-
cured by ex-   law, how to combine the maximum of
periment.   spiritual freedom with the maximum
of moral cohesion, is a problem for experiment
to solve. It cannot be solved, even ideally, in a
Utopia. For each interest in play has its rights
and the prophet neither knows what interests may
at a given future time subsist in the world, nor
what relative force they may have, nor what me-

chanical conditions may control their expression.
The statesman in his sphere and the individual
in his must find, as they go, the best practical solutions. All that can be indicated before-
hand is the principle which improvements in this
institution would comply with if they were really
improvements. They would reform and perfect
the function of reproduction without discarding
it; they would maintain the family unless they
could devise some institution that combined intrinsic and representative values better than does
that natural artifice, and they would recast either
the instincts or the laws concerned, or both simul-
taneously, until the family ceased to clash seriously with any of these three things: natural
affection, rational nurture, and moral freedom.

CHAPTER III

INDUSTRY, GOVERNMENT, AND WAR

Patriarchal economy. We have seen that the family, an association useful in rearing the young, may become a means of further maintenance and defence. It is the first economic and the first military group. Children become servants, and servants, being adopted and brought up in the family, become like other children and supply the family's growing wants. It was no small part of the extraordinary longing for progeny shown by patriarchal man that children were wealth, and that by continuing in life-long subjection to their father they lent prestige and power to his old age. The daughters drew water, the wives and concubines spun, wove, and prepared food. A great family was a great estate. It was augmented further by sheep, goats, asses, and cattle. This numerous household, bound together by personal authority and by common fortunes, was sufficient to carry on many rude industries. It wandered from pasture to pasture, practised hospitality, watched the stars, and seems (at least in poetic retrospect) to have been not unhappy. A Roman adage has declared that to know the world one household suffices; and one patriarchal family, in its simplicity and grandeur, seems to have given scope enough for almost all human virtues. And those early men, as Vico says, were sublime poets.

Origin of the state. Nevertheless, such a condition can only subsist in deserts where those who try to till the soil cannot grow strong enough to maintain themselves against marauding herdsmen. Whenever agriculture yields better returns and makes the husbandman rich enough to support a protector, patriarchal life disappears. The fixed occupation of land turns a tribe into a state. Plato has given the classic account of such a passage from idyllic to political conditions. Growth in population and in requirements forces an Arcadian community to encroach upon its neighbours; this encroachment means war; and war, when there are fields and granaries to protect, and slaves and artisans to keep at their domestic labours, means fortifications, an army, and a general. And to match the army in the field another must be maintained at home, composed of judges, priests, builders, cooks, barbers, and doctors. Such is the inception of what, in the literal sense of the word, may be called civilisation.

Civilisation secures three chief advantages: greater wealth, greater safety, and greater variety **Three uses of civilisation.** of experience. Whether, in spite of this, there is a real—that is, a moral —advance is a question impossible to answer offhand, because wealth, safety, and variety are not absolute goods, and their value is great or small according to the further values they may help to secure. This is obvious in the case of riches. But safety also is only good when there is something to preserve better than courage, and when the prolongation of life can serve to intensify its excellence. An animal's existence is not improved when made safe by imprisonment and domestication; it is only degraded and rendered passive and melancholy. The human savage likewise craves a freedom and many a danger inconsistent with civilisation, because independent of reason. He does not yet identify his interests with any persistent and ideal harmonies created by reflection. And when reflection is absent, length of life is no benefit: a quick succession of generations, with a small chance of reaching old age, is a beautiful thing in purely animal economy, where vigour is the greatest joy, propagation the highest function, and decrepitude the sorriest woe. The value of safety, accordingly, hangs on the question whether life has become reflective and rational. But the fact that a state arises does not in itself imply rationality. It makes rationality possible, but leaves it potential.

Its rationality contingent. Similar considerations apply to variety. To increase the number of instincts and functions is probably to produce confusion and to augment that secondary and reverberating kind of evil which consists in expecting pain and regretting misfortune. On the other hand, a perfect life could never be accused of monotony. All desirable variety lies within the circle of perfection. Thus we do not tire of possessing two legs nor wish, for the sake of variety, to be occasionally lunatics. Accordingly, an increase in variety of function is a good only if a unity can still be secured embracing that variety; otherwise it would have been better that the irrelevant function should have been developed by independent individuals or should not have arisen at all. The function of seeing double adds more to the variety than to the spice of life. Whether civilisation is a blessing depends, then, on its ulterior uses. Judged by those interests which already exist when it arises, it is very likely a burden and oppression. The birds' instinctive economy would not be benefited by a tax-gatherer, a recruiting-sergeant, a sect or two of theologians, and the other usual organs of human polity.

For the Life of Reason, however, civilisation is a necessary condition. Although animal life, within man and beyond him, has its wild beauty and mystic justifications, yet that specific form of life which we call rational, and which is no less natural than the rest, would never have arisen without an expansion of human faculty, an increase in mental scope, for which civilisation is necessary. Wealth, safety, variety of pursuits, are all requisite if memory and purpose are to be trained increasingly, and if a steadfast art of living is to supervene upon instinct and dream.

Sources of wealth.   Wealth is itself expressive of reason for it arises whenever men, instead of doing nothing or beating about casually in the world, take to gathering fruits of nature which they may have uses for in future, or fostering their growth, or actually contriving their appearance. Such is man's first industrial habit, seen in grazing, agriculture, and mining. Among nature's products are also those of man's own purposeless and imitative activity, results of his idle ingenuity and restlessness. Some of these, like nature's other random creations, may chance to have some utility. They may then become conspicuous to reflection, be strengthened by the relations which they establish in life, and be henceforth called works of human art. They then constitute a second industrial habit and that other sort of riches which is supplied by manufacture.

Excess of it possible.   The amount of wealth man can produce is apparently limited only by time, invention, and the material at hand. It can very easily exceed his capacity for enjoyment. As the habits which produce wealth were originally spontaneous and only crystallised into reasonable processes by mutual checks and the gradual settling down of the organism into harmonious action, so also the same habits may outrun their uses. The machinery to produce wealth, of which man's own energies have become a part, may well work on irrespective of happiness. Indeed, the industrial ideal would be an international commu-

nity with universal free trade, extreme division of
labour, and no unproductive consumption. Such
an arrangement would undoubtedly produce a
maximum of riches, and any objections made to
it, if intelligent, must be made on other than universal economic grounds. Free trade may be opposed, for instance (while patriotism takes the
invidious form of jealousy and while peace is not
secure), on the ground that it interferes with
vested interests and settled populations or with
national completeness and self-sufficiency, or that
absorption in a single industry is unfavourable to
intellectual life. The latter is also an obvious objection to any great division of labour, even in
liberal fields; while any man with a tender heart
and traditional prejudices might hesitate to condemn the irresponsible rich to extinction, together
with all paupers, mystics, and old maids living
on annuities.

Such attacks on industrialism, however, are
mere skirmishes and express prejudices of one sort
or another. The formidable judgment industrialism has to face is that of reason, which demands
that the increase and specification of labour be
justified by benefits somewhere actually realised
and integrated in individuals. Wealth must justify itself in happiness. Someone must live better
for having produced or enjoyed these possessions.
And he would not live better, even granting that
the possessions were in themselves advantages, if
these advantages were bought at too high a price

and removed other greater opportunities or benefits. The belle must not sit so long prinking before the glass as to miss the party, and man must
not work so hard and burden himself with so many
cares as to have no breath or interest left for
things free and intellectual. Work and life too
often are contrasted and complementary things;
but they would not be contrasted nor even sepa-
rable if work were not servile, for of course man
can have no life save in occupation, and in the
exercise of his faculties; contemplation itself can
deal only with what practice contains or discloses.
But the pursuit of wealth is a pursuit of instruments. The division of labour when extreme does
violence to natural genius and obliterates natural
distinctions in capacity. What is properly called
industry is not art or self-justifying activity, but
on the contrary a distinctly compulsory and merely instrumental labour, which if justified at all
must be justified by some ulterior advantage which
it secures. In regard to such instrumental activities the question is always pertinent whether they
do not produce more than is useful, or prevent
the existence of something that is intrinsically
good.

Occidental society has evidently run in this direction into great abuses, complicating
life prodigiously without ennobling the
mind. It has put into rich men's hands facilities
and luxuries which they trifle with without achiev-
ing any dignity or true magnificence in living,

Irrational in-
dustry.

while the poor, if physically more comfortable than formerly, are not meantime notably wiser or merrier. Ideal distinction has been sacrificed in the best men, to add material comforts to the worst. Things, as Emerson said, are in the saddle and ride mankind. The means crowd out the ends and civilisation reverts, when it least thinks it, to barbarism.

The acceptable side of industrialism, which is **Its jovial and** supposed to be inspired exclusively by **ingenious side.** utility, is not utility at all but pure achievement. If we wish to do such an age justice we must judge it as we should a child and praise its feats without inquiring after its purposes. That is its own spirit: a spirit dominant at the present time, particularly in America, where industrialism appears most free from alloy. There is a curious delight in turning things over, changing their shape, discovering their possibilities, making of them some new contrivance. Use, in these experimental minds, as in nature, is only incidental. There is an irrational creative impulse, a zest in novelty, in progression, in beating the other man, or, as they say, in breaking the record. There is also a fascination in seeing the world unbosom itself of ancient secrets, obey man's coaxing, and take on unheard-of shapes. The highest building, the largest steamer, the fastest train, the book reaching the widest circulation have, in America, a clear title to respect. When the just functions of things are as yet not discriminated, the superlative in any direction seems naturally admirable. Again, many possessions, if they do not make a man better, are at least expected to make his children happier; and this pathetic hope is behind many exertions. An experimental materialism, spontaneous and divorced from reason and from everything useful, is also confused in some minds with traditional duties; and a school of popular hierophants is not lacking that turns it into a sort of religion and perhaps calls it idealism. Impulse is more visible in all this than purpose, imagination more than judgment; but it is pleasant for the moment to abound in invention and effort and to let the future cash the account.

Wealth is excessive when it reduces a man to a middleman and a jobber, when it prevents him, in his preoccupation with material things, from making his spirit the measure of them. There are Nibelungen who toil underground over a gold they will never use, and in their obsession with production begrudge themselves all holidays, all concessions to inclination, to merriment, to fancy; nay, they would even curtail as much as possible the free years of their youth, when they might see the blue, before rendering up their souls to the Leviathan. Visible signs of such unreason soon appear in the relentless and hideous aspect which life puts on; for those instruments which somehow emancipate themselves from their uses soon become hateful. In nature irresponsible wildness can be turned

Its tyranny.

to beauty, because every product can be recom-
posed into some abstract manifestation of force
or form; but the monstrous in man himself and
in his works immediately offends, for here everything is expected to symbolise its moral relations.
The irrational in the human has something about
it altogether repulsive and terrible, as we see in
the maniac, the miser, the drunkard, or the ape.
A barbaric civilisation, built on blind impulse and
ambition, should fear to awaken a deeper detesta-
tion than could ever be aroused by those more
beautiful tyrannies, chivalrous or religious, against
which past revolutions have been directed.

An impossible remedy. Both the sordidness and the luxury
which industrialism may involve, could
be remedied, however, by a better distribution of
the product. The riches now created by labour
would probably not seriously debauch mankind
if each man had only his share; and such a proportionate return would enable him to perceive
directly how far his interests required him to
employ himself in material production and how
far he could allow himself leisure for spontaneous things—religion, play, art, study, conversation. In a world composed entirely of philosophers an hour or two a day of manual labour—a
very welcome quantity—would provide for material wants; the rest could then be all the more
competently dedicated to a liberal life; for a
healthy soul needs matter quite as much for an
object of interest as for a means of sustenance.

But philosophers do not yet people nor even govern the world, and so simple a Utopia which reason, if it had direct efficacy, would long ago have reduced to act, is made impossible by the cross-currents of instinct, tradition, and fancy which variously deflect affairs.

Basis of government.   What are called the laws of nature are so many observations made by man on a way things have of repeating themselves by replying always to their old causes and never, as reason's prejudice would expect, to their new opportunities. This inertia, which physics registers in the first law of motion, natural history and psychology call habit. Habit is a physical law. It is the basis and force of all morality, but is not morality itself. In society it takes the form of custom which, when codified, is called law and when enforced is called government. Government is the political representative of a natural equilibrium, of custom, of inertia; it is by no means a representative of reason. But, like any mechanical complication, it may become rational, and many of its forms and operations may be defended on rational grounds. All natural organisms, from protoplasm to poetry, can exercise certain ideal functions and symbolise in their structure certain ideal relations. Protoplasm tends to propagate itself, and in so doing may turn into a conscious ideal the end it already tends to realise; but there could be no desire for self-preservation were there not already a self pre-

served. So government can by its existence define
the commonwealth it tends to preserve, and its
acts may be approved from the point of view of
those eventual interests which they satisfy. But
government neither subsists nor arises because it
is good or useful, but solely because it is inevitable.
It becomes good in so far as the inevitable adjustment of political forces which it embodies is also
a just provision for all the human interests which
it creates or affects.

Suppose a cold and hungry savage, failing to
find berries and game enough in the woods, should
descend into some meadow where a flock of sheep
were grazing and pounce upon a lame lamb which
could not run away with the others, tear its flesh,
suck up its blood, and dress himself in its skin.
All this could not be called an affair undertaken
in the sheep's interest. And yet it might well
conduce to their interest in the end. For the
How rational- savage, finding himself soon hungry
ity accrues. again, and insufficiently warm in that
scanty garment, might attack the flock a second
time, and thereby begin to accustom himself, and
also his delighted family, to a new and more substantial sort of raiment and diet. Suppose, now,
a pack of wolves, or a second savage, or a dis-
ease should attack those unhappy sheep. Would
not their primeval enemy defend them? Would
he not have identified himself with their interests to this extent, that their total extinction
or discomfiture would alarm him also? And in

so far as he provided for their well-being, would he not have become a good shepherd? If, now, some philosophic wether, a lover of his kind, reasoned with his fellows upon the change in their condition, he might shudder indeed at those early episodes and at the contribution of lambs and fleeces which would not cease to be levied by the new government; but he might also consider that such a contribution was nothing in comparison with what was formerly exacted by wolves, diseases, frosts, and casual robbers, when the flock was much smaller than it had now grown to be, and much less able to withstand decimation. And he might even have conceived an admiration for the remarkable wisdom and beauty of that great shepherd, dressed in such a wealth of wool; and he might remember pleasantly some occasional caress received from him and the daily trough filled with water by his providential hand. And he might not be far from maintaining not only the rational origin, but the divine right of shepherds.

Such a savage enemy, incidentally turned into a useful master, is called a conqueror or king. Only in human experience the case is not so simple and harmony is seldom established so quickly. The history of Asia is replete with examples of conquest and extortion in which a rural population living in comparative plenty is attacked by some more ferocious neighbour who, after a round of pillage, establishes a quite unnecessary government, raising taxes and soldiers for purposes absolutely remote from the conquered people's interests. Such a government is nothing but a chronic raid, mitigated by the desire to leave the inhabitants prosperous enough to be continually despoiled afresh. Even this modicum of protection, however, can establish a certain moral bond between ruler and subject; an intelligent government and an intelligent fealty become conceivable.

Ferocious but useful despotisms. Not only may the established régime be superior to any other that could be substituted for it at the time, but some security against total destruction, and a certain opportunity for the arts and for personal advancement may follow subjugation. A moderate decrease in personal independence may be compensated by a novel public grandeur; palace and temple may make amends for hovels somewhat more squalid than before. Hence, those who cannot conceive a rational polity, or a co-operative greatness in the state, especially if they have a luxurious fancy, can take pleasure in despotism; for it does not, after all, make so much difference to an ordinary fool whether what he suffers from is another's oppression or his own lazy improvidence; and he can console himself by saying with Goldsmith:

> How small, of all that human hearts endure,
> The part which laws or kings can cause or cure.

At the same time a court and a hierarchy, with their interesting pomp and historic continuity, with their combined appeal to greed and imagination, redeem human existence from pervasive vulgarity and allow somebody at least to strut proudly over the earth. Serfs are not in a worse material condition than savages, and their spiritual opportunities are infinitely greater; for their eye and fancy are fed with visions of human greatness, and even if they cannot improve their outward estate they can possess a poetry and a religion. It suffices to watch an Oriental rabble at prayer, or listening in profound immobility to some wandering story-teller or musician, to feel how much such a people may have to ruminate upon, and how truly Arabian days and Arabian Nights go together. The ideas evolved may be wild and futile and the emotions savagely sensuous, yet they constitute a fund of inner experience, a rich soil for better imaginative growths. To such Oriental cogitations, for instance, carried on under the shadow of uncontrollable despotisms, mankind owes all its greater religions.

A government's origin has nothing to do with its legitimacy; that is, with its representative operation. An absolutism based on conquest or on religious fraud may wholly lose its hostile function. It may become the nucleus of a national organisation expressing justly enough the people's requirements. Such a representative character is harder to attain when the government is foreign, for diversity in race language and local ties makes the ruler less apt involuntarily to represent his

subjects; his measures must subserve their interests intentionally, out of sympathy, policy, and a
sense of duty, virtues which are seldom efficacious
for any continuous period. A native government,
even if based on initial outrage, can more easily
drift into excellence; for when a great man mounts
the throne he has only to read his own soul and
follow his instinctive ambitions in order to make
himself the leader and spokesman of his nation.
An Alexander, an Alfred, a Peter the Great, are
examples of persons who with varying degrees of
virtue were representative rulers: their policy,
however irrationally inspired, happened to serve
their subjects and the world. Besides, a native
government is less easily absolute. Many influences control the ruler in his aims and habits,
such as religion, custom, and the very language
he speaks, by which praise and blame are assigned
automatically to the objects loved or hated by the
people. He cannot, unless he be an intentional
monster, oppose himself wholly to the common
soul.

For this very reason, however, native governments are little fitted to redeem or
Occasional ad-
vantage of be- transform a people, and all great up-
ing conquered. heavals and regenerations have been
brought about by conquest, by the substitution of
one race and spirit for another in the counsels
of the world. What the Orient owes to Greece,
the Occident to Rome, India to England, native
America to Spain, is a civilisation incomparably

better than that which the conquered people could ever have provided for themselves. Conquest is a good means of recasting those ideals, perhaps impracticable and ignorant, which a native government at its best would try to preserve. Such inapt ideals, it is true, would doubtless remodel themselves if they could be partly realised. Progress from within is possible, otherwise no progress would be possible for humanity at large. But conquest gives at once a freer field to those types of polity which, since they go with strength, presumably represent the better adjustment to natural conditions, and therefore the better ideal. Though the substance of ideals is the will, their mould must be experience and a true discernment of opportunity; so that while all ideals, regarded *in vacuo*, are equal in ideality, they are, under given circumstances, very diverse in worth.

Origin of free governments. When not founded on conquest, which is the usual source of despotism, government is ordinarily based on traditional authority vested in elders or patriarchal kings. This is the origin of the classic state, and of all aristocracy and freedom. The economic and political unit is a great household with its lord, his wife and children, clients and slaves. In the interstices of these households there may be a certain floating residuum—freedmen, artisans, merchants, strangers. These people, while free, are without such rights as even slaves possess; they have no share in the religion, education, and re-

sources of any established family. For purposes
of defence and religion the heads of houses gather
together in assemblies, elect or recognise some
chief, and agree upon laws, usually little more
than extant customs regulated and formally sanc-
tioned.

Such a state tends to expand in two directions.
In the first place, it becomes more democratic;
that is, it tends to recognise other influences than that which heads of families—*patres conscripti*—possess. The
people without such fathers, those who are not
patricians, also have children and come to imitate
on a smaller scale the patriarchal economy. These
plebeians are admitted to citizenship. But they
have no such religious dignity and power in their
little families as the patricians have in theirs; they
are scarcely better than loose individuals, representing nothing but their own sweet wills. This
individualism and levity is not, however, confined
to the plebeians; it extends to the patrician
houses. Individualism is the second direction in
which a patriarchal society yields to innovation.
As the state grows the family weakens; and while
in early Rome, for instance, only the *pater familias*
was responsible to the city, and his children and
slaves only to him, in Greece we find from early
times individuals called to account before public
judges. A federation of households thus became
a republic. The king, that chief who enjoyed a
certain hereditary precedence in sacrifices or in

Their demo-
cratic tenden-
cies.

war, yields to elected generals and magistrates whose power, while it lasts, is much greater; for no other comparable power now subsists in the levelled state.

Modern Europe has seen an almost parallel development of democracy and individualism, together with the establishment of great artificial governments. Though the feudal hierarchy was originally based on conquest or domestic subjection, it came to have a fanciful or chivalrous or political force. But gradually the plebeian classes—the burghers—grew in importance, and military allegiance was weakened by being divided between a number of superposed lords, up to the king, emperor, or pope. The stronger rulers grew into absolute monarchs, representatives of great states, and the people became, in a political sense, a comparatively level multitude. Where parliamentary government was established it became possible to subordinate or exclude the monarch and his court; but the government remains an involuntary institution, and the individual must adapt himself to its exigencies. The church which once overshadowed the state has now lost its coercive authority and the single man stands alone before an impersonal written law, a constitutional government, and a widely diffused and contagious public opinion, characterised by enormous inertia, incoherence, and blindness. Contemporary national units are strongly marked and stimulate on occasion a perfervid artificial patriotism; but they are strangely unrepresentative of either personal or universal interests and may yield in turn to new combinations, if the industrial and intellectual solidarity of mankind, every day more obvious, ever finds a fit organ to express and to defend it.

A despotic military government founded on alien force and aiming at its own magnificence is often more efficient in defending its subjects than is a government expressing only the people's energies, as the predatory shepherd and his dog prove better guardians for a flock than its own wethers. The robbers that at their first incursion brought terror to merchant and peasant may become almost immediately representative organs of society—an army and a judiciary. Disputes between subjects are naturally submitted to the invader, under whose laws and good-will alone a practical settlement can now be effected; and this alien tribunal, being exempt from local prejudices and interested in peace that taxes may be undiminished, may administer a comparatively impartial justice, until corrupted by bribes. The constant compensation tyranny brings, which keeps it from at once exhausting its victims, is the silence it imposes on their private squabbles. One distant universal enemy is less oppressive than a thousand unchecked pilferers and plotters at home. For this reason the reader of ancient history so often has occasion to remark what immense prosperity

Imperial peace.

Asiatic provinces enjoyed between the periods
when their successive conquerors devastated
them. They flourished exceedingly the moment
peace and a certain order were established in
them.

Tyranny not only protects the subject against
his kinsmen, thus taking on the functions of law
and police, but it also protects him against military invasion, and thus takes on the function of
an army. An army, considered

Nominal and real status of armies. ideally, is an organ for the state's
protection; but it is far from being
such in its origin, since at first an army is nothing
but a ravenous and lusty horde quartered in a
conquered country; yet the cost of such an incu-
bus may come to be regarded as an insurance
against further attack, and so what is in its real
basis an inevitable burden resulting from a
chance balance of forces may be justified in after-
thought as a rational device for defensive purposes. Such an ulterior justification has nothing
to do, however, with the causes that maintain
armies or military policies: and accordingly those
virginal minds that think things originated in the
uses they may have acquired, have frequent cause
to be pained and perplexed at the abuses and over-
development of militarism. An insurance capi-
talised may exceed the value of the property
insured, and the drain caused by armies and
navies may be much greater than the havoc they
prevent. The evils against which they are sup-

posed to be directed are often evils only in a cant
and conventional sense, since the events depre-
cated (like absorption by a neighbouring state)
might be in themselves no misfortune to the people, but perhaps a singular blessing. And those
dreaded possibilities, even if really evil, may well
be less so than is the hateful actuality of military
taxes, military service, and military arrogance.

Their action ir-
responsible. Nor is this all: the military classes,
since they inherit the blood and habits
of conquerors, naturally love war and their irrational combativeness is reinforced by interest; for
in war officers can shine and rise, while the danger
of death, to a brave man, is rather a spur and
a pleasing excitement than a terror. A military
class is therefore always recalling, foretelling,
and meditating war; it fosters artificial and senseless jealousies toward other governments that
possess armies; and finally, as often as not, it
precipitates disaster by bringing about the objectless struggle on which it has set its heart.

These natural phenomena, unintelligently regarded as anomalies and abuses, are the appanage
Pugnacity hu- of war in its pristine and proper form.
man. To fight is a radical instinct; if men
have nothing else to fight over they will fight
over words, fancies, or women, or they will fight
because they dislike each other's looks, or
because they have met walking in opposite directions. To knock a thing down, especially if it
is cocked at an arrogant angle, is a deep delight

to the blood. To fight for a reason and in a calculating spirit is something your true warrior despises; even a coward might screw his courage up to such a reasonable conflict. The joy and glory of fighting lie in its pure spontaneity and consequent generosity; you are not fighting for gain, but for sport and for victory. Victory, no doubt, has its fruits for the victor. If fighting were not a possible means of livelihood the bellicose instinct could never have established itself in any long-lived race. A few men can live on plunder, just as there is room in the world for some beasts of prey; other men are reduced to living on industry, just as there are diligent bees, ants, and herbivorous kine. But victory need have no good fruits for the people whose army is victorious. That it sometimes does so is an ulterior and blessed circumstance hardly to be reckoned upon.

Since barbarism has its pleasures it naturally **Barrack-room** has its apologists. There are pane- **philosophy.** gyrists of war who say that without a periodical bleeding a race decays and loses its manhood. Experience is directly opposed to this shameless assertion. It is war that wastes a nation's wealth, chokes its industries, kills its flower, narrows its sympathies, condemns it to be governed by adventurers, and leaves the puny, deformed, and unmanly to breed the next generation. Internecine war, foreign and civil, brought about the greatest set-back which the

Life of Reason has ever suffered; it exterminated the Greek and Italian aristocracies. Instead of being descended from heroes, modern nations are descended from slaves; and it is not their bodies only that show it. After a long peace, if the conditions of life are propitious, we observe a people's energies bursting their barriers; they become aggressive on the strength they have stored up in their remote and unchecked development. It is the unmutilated race, fresh from the struggle with nature (in which the best survive, while in war it is often the best that perish) that descends victoriously into the arena of nations and conquers disciplined armies at the first blow, becomes the military aristocracy of the next epoch and is itself ultimately sapped and decimated by luxury and battle, and merged at last into the ignoble conglomerate beneath. Then, perhaps, in some other virgin country a genuine humanity is again found, capable of victory because unbled by war. To call war the soil of courage and virtue is like calling debauchery the soil of love.

Military institutions, adventitious and ill-adapted excrescences as they usually are, can acquire rational values in various ways. Besides occasional defence, they furnish a profession congenial to many, and a spectacle and emotion interesting to all. Blind courage is **Military virtues.** an animal virtue indispensable in a world full of dangers and evils where a certain insensibility and dash are requisite to

skirt the precipice without vertigo. Such animal
courage seems therefore beautiful rather than
desperate or cruel, and being the lowest and most
instinctive of virtues it is the one most widely
and sincerely admired. In the form of steadiness
under risks rationally taken, and perseverance so
long as there is a chance of success, courage is a
true virtue; but it ceases to be one when the love
of danger, a useful passion when danger is un-
avoidable, begins to lead men into evils which it
was unnecessary to face. Bravado, provocative-
ness, and a gambler's instinct, with a love of
hitting hard for the sake of exercise, is a temper
which ought already to be counted among the
vices rather than the virtues of man. To delight
in war is a merit in the soldier, a dangerous quality in the captain, and a positive crime in the
statesman.

Discipline, or the habit of obedience, is a better
sort of courage which military life also requires.
Discipline is the acquired faculty of surrendering an immediate personal good for the sake of
a remote and impersonal one of greater value.
This difficult wisdom is made easier by training
in an army, because the great forces of habit,
example and social suasion, are there enlisted in
its service. But these natural aids make it lose
its conscious rationality, so that it ceases to be
a virtue except potentially; for to resist an impulse by force of habit or external command may
or may not be to follow the better course.

Besides fostering these rudimentary virtues the army gives the nation's soul its most festive and flaunting embodiment. Popular heroes, stirring episodes, obvious turning-points in history, commonly belong to military life.

They are splendid vices. Nevertheless the panegyrist of war places himself on the lowest level on which a moralist or patriot can stand and shows as great a want of refined feeling as of right reason. For the glories of war are all bloodstained, delirious, and infected with crime; the combative instinct is a savage prompting by which one man's good is found in another's evil. The existence of such a contradiction in the moral world is the original sin of nature, whence flows every other wrong. He is a willing accomplice of that perversity in things who delights in another's discomfiture or in his own, and craves the blind tension of plunging into danger without reason, or the idiot's pleasure in facing a pure chance. To find joy in another's trouble is, as man is constituted, not unnatural, though it is wicked; and to find joy in one's own trouble, though it be madness, is not yet impossible for man. These are the chaotic depths of that dreaming nature out of which humanity has to grow.

Absolute value in strife. If war could be abolished and the defence of all interests intrusted to courts of law, there would remain unsatisfied a primary and therefore ineradicable instinct—a love of conflict, of rivalry, and of victory. If

we desire to abolish war because it tries to do
good by doing harm, we must not ourselves do
an injury to human nature while trying to smooth
it out. Now the test and limit of all necessary
reform is vital harmony. No impulse can be
condemned arbitrarily or because some other impulse or group of interests is, in a Platonic way,
out of sympathy with it. An instinct can be condemned only if it prevents the realisation of other
instincts, and only in so far as it does so. War,
which has instinctive warrant, must therefore be
transformed only in so far as it does harm to
other interests. The evils of war are obvious
enough; could not the virtues of war, animal courage, discipline, and self-knowledge, together with
gaiety and enthusiasm, find some harmless occasion for their development?

Such a harmless simulacrum of war is seen in
sport. The arduous and competitive
element in sport is not harmful, if the
discipline involved brings no loss of
faculty or of right sensitiveness, and the rivalry
no rancour. In war states wish to be efficient in
order to conquer, but in sport men wish to prove
their excellence because they wish to have it. If
this excellence does not exist, the aim is missed,
and to discover that failure is no new misfortune.
To have failed unwittingly would have been worse;
and to recognise superiority in another is consistent with a relatively good and honourable performance, so that even nominal failure may be a

Sport a civil-
ised way of
preserving it.

substantial success. And merit in a rival should
bring a friendly delight even to the vanquished
if they are true lovers of sport and of excellence.
Sport is a liberal form of war stripped of its com-
pulsions and malignity; a rational art and the
expression of a civilised instinct.

The abolition of war, like its inception, can only
be brought about by a new collocation
Who shall found the universal commonwealth? of material forces. As the suppression of some nest of piratical tribes by
a great emperor substitutes judicial
for military sanctions among them, so the conquest of all warring nations by some imperial people could alone establish general peace. The
Romans approached this ideal because their vast
military power stood behind their governors and
prætors. Science and commerce might conceivably resume that lost imperial function. If at the
present day two or three powerful governments
could so far forget their irrational origin as to
renounce the right to occasional piracy and could
unite in enforcing the decisions of some international tribunal, they would thereby constitute that
tribunal the organ of a universal government and
render war impossible between responsible states.
But on account of their irrational basis all governments largely misrepresent the true interests of
those who live under them. They pursue conventional and captious ends to which alone public
energies can as yet be efficiently directed.

CHAPTER IV

THE ARISTOCRATIC IDEAL

Eminence, once existing, grows by its own operation. " To him that hath shall be given," says the Gospel, representing as a principle of divine justice one that undoubtedly holds in earthly economy. A not dissimilar observation is made in the proverb: " Possession is nine-tenths of the law." Indeed, some trifling acquisition often gives an animal an initial advantage which may easily roll up and increase prodigiously, becoming the basis of prolonged good fortune. Sometimes this initial advantage is a matter of natural structure, like talent, strength, or goodness; sometimes an accidental accretion, like breeding, instruction, or wealth. Such advantages grow by the opportunities they make; and it is possible for a man launched into the world at the right moment with the right equipment to mount easily from eminence to eminence and accomplish very great things without doing more than genially follow his instincts and respond with ardour, like an Alexander or a Shakespeare, to his opportunities. A great endowment, doubled by great good for-

tune, raises men like these into supreme representatives of mankind.

It is no loss of liberty to subordinate ourselves
to a natural leader. On the contrary, we thereby
seize an opportunity to exercise our freedom, avail-
ing ourselves of the best instrument obtainable to
accomplish our ends. A man may be a natural
leader either by his character or by his
position. The advantages a man draws
from that peculiar structure of his
brain which renders him, for instance, a ready
speaker or an ingenious mathematician, are by
common consent regarded as legitimate advantages. The public will use and reward such ability without jealousy and with positive delight. In
an unsophisticated age the same feeling prevails
in regard to those advantages which a man may
draw from more external circumstances. If a
traveller, having been shipwrecked in some expe-
dition, should learn the secrets of an unknown
land, its arts and resources, his fellow-citizens,
on his return, would not hesitate to follow his
direction in respect to those novel matters. It
would be senseless folly on their part to begrudge
him his adventitious eminence and refuse to es-
teem him of more consequence than their unin-
itiated selves. Yet when people, ignoring the natural causes of all that is called artificial, think
that but for an unlucky chance they, too, might
have enjoyed the advantages which raise other
men above them, they sometimes affect not to rec-

*Its causes nat-
ural and its
privileges just.*

ognise actual distinctions and abilities, or study enviously the means of annulling them. So long, however, as by the operation of any causes whatever some real competence accrues to anyone, it is for the general interest that this competence should bear its natural fruits, diversifying the face of society and giving its possessor a corresponding distinction.

Variety in the world is an unmixed blessing so **Advantage of inequality.** long as each distinct function can be exercised without hindrance to any other. There is no greater stupidity or meanness than to take uniformity for an ideal, as if it were not a benefit and a joy to a man, being what he is, to know that many are, have been, and will be better than he. Grant that no one is positively degraded by the great man's greatness and it follows that everyone is exalted by it. Beauty, genius, holiness, even power and extraordinary wealth, radiate their virtue and make the world in which they exist a better and a more joyful place to live in. Hence the insatiable vulgar curiosity about great people, and the strange way in which the desire for fame (by which the distinguished man sinks to the common level) is met and satisfied by the universal interest in whatever is extraordinary. This avidity not to miss knowledge of things notable, and to enact vicariously all singular rôles, shows the need men have of distinction and the advantage they find even in conceiving it. For it is the presence of variety

and a nearer approach somewhere to just and ideal
achievement that gives men perspective in their
judgments and opens vistas from the dull fore-
ground of their lives to sea, mountain, and stars.

No merely idle curiosity shows itself in this
instinct; rather a mark of human potentiality that
recognises in what is yet attained a sad caricature
of what is essentially attainable. For man's spirit
is intellectual and naturally demands dominion
and science; it craves in all things friendliness
and beauty. The least hint of attainment in these
directions fills it with satisfaction and the sense
of realised expectation. So much so that when
no inkling of a supreme fulfilment is found in
the world or in the heart, men still cling to the
notion of it in God or the hope of it in heaven,
and religion, when it entertains them with that
ideal, seems to have reached its highest height.
Love of uniformity would quench the thirst for
new outlets, for perfect, even if alien, achievements, and this, so long as perfection had not
been actually attained, would indicate a mind
dead to the ideal.

Menenius Agrippa expressed very well the aristocratic theory of society when he
compared the state to a human body
in which the common people were the
hands and feet, and the nobles the belly. The
people, when they forgot the conditions of their
own well-being, might accuse themselves of folly
and the nobles of insolent idleness, for the poor

Fable of the belly and the members.

spent their lives in hopeless labour that others
who did nothing might enjoy all. But there was
a secret circulation of substance in the body politic, and the focussing of all benefits in the few
was the cause of nutrition and prosperity to the
many. Perhaps the truth might be even better
expressed in a physiological figure somewhat more
modern, by saying that the brain, which consumes
much blood, well repays its obligations to the
stomach and members, for it co-ordinates their
motions and prepares their satisfactions. Yet
there is this important difference between the
human body and the state, a difference which
renders Agrippa's fable wholly misleading: the
Fallacy in it. hands and feet have no separate consciousness, and if they are ill used it is
the common self that feels the weariness and the
bruises. But in the state the various members
have a separate sensibility, and, although their ultimate interests lie, no doubt, in co-operation and
justice, their immediate instinct and passion may
lead them to oppress one another perpetually. At
one time the brain, forgetting the members, may
feast on opiates and unceasing music; and again,
the members, thinking they could more econom-
ically shift for themselves, may starve the brain
and reduce the body politic to a colony of vege-
tating microbes. In a word, the consciousness in-
habiting the brain embodies the functions of all
the body's organs, and responds in a general way
to all their changes of fortune, but in the state

every cell has a separate brain, and the greatest citizen, by his existence, realises only his own happiness.

For an ideal aristocracy we should not look to Plato's Republic, for that Utopia is avowedly the ideal only for fallen and corrupt states, since luxury and injustice, we are told, first necessitated war, and the guiding idea of all the Platonic regimen is military efficiency. Aristocracy finds a more ideal expression in theism; for theism imagines the values of existence to be divided into two unequal parts: on the one hand the infinite value of God's life, on the other the finite values of all the created hierarchy. According to theistic cosmology, there was a metaphysical necessity, if creatures were to exist at all, that they should be in some measure inferior to godhead; otherwise they would have been indistinguishable from the godhead itself according to the principle called the identity of indiscernibles, which declares that two beings exactly alike cannot exist without collapsing into an undivided unit. The propagation of life involved, then, declension from pure vitality, and to diffuse being meant to dilute it with nothingness. This declension might take place in infinite degrees, each retaining some vestige of perfection mixed, as it were, with a greater and greater proportion of impotence and nonentity. Below God stood the angels, below them man, and below man the brute and inanimate creation. Each

[margin note: Theism expresses better the aristocratic ideal.]

sphere, as it receded, contained a paler adumbration of the central perfection; yet even at the last confines of existence some feeble echo of divinity would still resound. This inequality in dignity would be not only a beauty in the whole, to whose existence and order such inequalities would be essential, but also no evil to the creature and no injustice; for a modicum of good is not made evil simply because a greater good is elsewhere possible. On the contrary, by accepting that appointed place and that specific happiness, each servant of the universal harmony could feel its infinite value and could thrill the more profoundly to a music which he helped to intone.

A heaven with many man-sions. Dante has expressed this thought with great simplicity and beauty. He asks a friend's spirit, which he finds lodged in the lowest circle of paradise, if a desire to mount higher does not sometimes visit him; and the spirit replies:

" Brother, the force of charity quiets our will, making us wish only for what we have and thirst for nothing more. If we desired to be in a sublimer sphere, our desires would be discordant with the will of him who here allots us our divers stations—something which you will see there is no room for in these circles, if to dwell in charity be needful here, and if you consider duly the nature of charity. For it belongs to the essence of that blessed state to keep within the divine purposes, that our own purposes may become one also.

Thus, the manner in which we are ranged from step to step in this kingdom pleases the whole kingdom, as it does the king who gives us will to will with him. And his will is our peace; it is that sea toward which all things move that his will creates and that nature fashions." *

Such pious resignation has in it something pa-
thetic and constrained, which Dante could not or would not disguise. For a theism which, like Aristotle's and Dante's, has a Platonic essence, God is really nothing but the goal of human aspiration embodied imaginatively. This fact makes these philosophers feel that whatever falls short of divinity has something imperfect about it. God is what man ought to be; and man, while he is still himself, must yearn for ever, like Aristotle's cosmos, making in his perpetual round a vain imitation of deity, and an eternal prayer. Hence, a latent minor strain in Aristotle's philosophy, the hopeless note of paganism, and in Dante an undertone of sorrow and sacrifice, inseparable from Christian feeling. In both, virtue implies a certain sense of defeat, a fatal unnatural limitation, as if a pristine ideal had been surrendered and what remained were at best a compromise. Accordingly we need not be surprised if aspiration, in all these men, finally takes a mystical turn; and Dante's ghostly friends, after propounding their aristocratic philosophy, to justify God in other men's eyes,

If God is defined as the human ideal, apotheosis the only paradise.

* Paradiso.   Canto III., 70-87.

are themselves on the point of quitting the lower
sphere to which God had assigned them and plunging into the " sea " of his absolute ecstasy. For,
if the word God stands for man's spiritual ideal,
heaven can consist only in apotheosis. This the
Greeks knew very well. They instinctively ignored
or feared any immortality which fell short of deifi-
cation ; and the Christian mystics reached the same
goal by less overt courses. They merged the popular idea of a personal God in their foretaste of
peace and perfection ; and their whole religion was
an effort to escape humanity.

When natures differ perfections differ too. It is true that the theistic cosmology might bear a different interpreta-
tion. If by deity we mean not man's
ideal—intellectual or sensuous—but the total cosmic order, then the universal hierarchy may be understood naturalistically so that each sphere gives
scope for one sort of good. God, or the highest
being, would then be simply the life of nature as
a whole, if nature has a conscious life, or that of
its noblest portion. The supposed " metaphysical
evil " involved in finitude would then be no evil
at all, but the condition of every good. In real-
ising his own will in his own way, each creature
would be perfectly happy, without yearning or
pathetic regrets for other forms of being. Such
forms of being would all be unpalatable to him,
even if conventionally called higher, because their
body was larger, and their soul more complex.
Nor would divine perfection itself be in any sense

perfection unless it gave expression to some definite nature, the entelechy either of the celestial spheres, or of scientific thought, or of some other actual existence. Under these circumstances, inhabitants even of the lowest heaven would be unreservedly happy, as happy in their way as those of the seventh heaven could be in theirs. No pathetic note would any longer disquiet their finitude. They would not have to renounce, in sad conformity to an alien will, what even for them would have been a deeper joy. They would be asked to renounce nothing but what, for them, would be an evil. The overruling providence would then in truth be fatherly, by providing for each being that which it inwardly craved. Persons of one rank would not be improved by passing into the so-called higher sphere, any more than the ox would be improved by being transformed into a lark, or a king into a poet.

Man in such a system could no more pine to be God than he could pine to be the law of gravity, or Spinoza's substance, or Hegel's dialectical idea. Such naturalistic abstractions, while they perhaps express some element of reality or its total form, are not objects corresponding to man's purposes and are morally inferior to his humanity. Every man's ideal lies within the potentialities of his nature, for only by expressing his nature can ideals possess authority or attraction over him. Heaven accordingly has really many mansions, each truly heavenly to him who would inhabit it, and there is really no room for discord in those rounds. One ideal can no more conflict with another than truth can jostle truth; but men, or the disorganised functions within a given individual, may be in physical conflict, as opinion may wrestle with opinion in the world's arena or in an ignorant brain. Among ideals themselves infinite variety is consistent with perfect harmony, but matter that has not yet developed or discovered its organic affinities may well show groping and contradictory tendencies. When, however, these embryonic disorders are once righted, each possible life knows its natural paradise, and what some unintelligent outsider might say in dispraise of that ideal will never wound or ruffle the self-justified creature whose ideal it is, any more than a cat's aversion to water will disturb a fish's plan of life.

An aristocratic society might accordingly be a perfect heaven if the variety and su-
Theory that stations actually correspond to faculty.
perposition of functions in it expressed a corresponding diversity in its members' faculties and ideals. And, indeed, what aristocratic philosophers have always maintained is that men really differ so much in capacity that one is happier for being a slave, another for being a shopkeeper, and a third for being a king. All professions, they say, even the lowest, are or may be vocations. Some men, Aristotle tells us, are slaves by nature; only physical functions are spontaneous in them. So long as

they are humanely treated, it is, we may infer, a benefit for them to be commanded; and the contribution their labour makes toward rational life in their betters is the highest dignity they can attain, and should be prized by them as a sufficient privilege.

Such assertions, coming from lordly lips, have a suspicious optimism about them; yet the faithful slave, such as the nurse we find in the tragedies, may sometimes have corresponded to that description. In other regions it is surely true that to advance in conventional station would often entail a loss in true dignity and happiness. It would seldom benefit a musician to be appointed admiral or a housemaid to become a prima donna. Scientific breeding might conceivably develop much more sharply the various temperaments and faculties needed in the state; and then each caste or order of citizens would not be more commonly dissatisfied with its lot than men or women now are with their sex. One tribe would run errands as persistently as the ants; another would sing like the lark; a third would show a devil's innate fondness for stoking a fiery furnace.

Aristocracy logically involves castes. But such castes as exist in India, and the social classes we find in the western world, are not now **Its falsity.** based on any profound difference in race, capacity, or inclination. They are based probably on the chances of some early war, reinforced by custom and perpetuated by inheritance.

A certain circulation, corresponding in part to proved ability or disability, takes place in the body politic, and, since the French Revolution, has taken place increasingly. Some, by energy and perseverance, rise from the bottom; some, by ill fortune or vice, fall from the top. But these readjustments are insignificant in comparison with the social inertia that perpetuates all the classes, and even such shifts as occur at once re-establish artificial conditions for the next generation. As a rule, men's station determines their occupation without their gifts determining their station. Thus stifled ability in the lower orders, and apathy or pampered incapacity in the higher, unite to deprive society of its natural leaders.

It would be easy, however, to exaggerate the havoc wrought by such artificial conditions. The monotony we observe in mankind must not be charged to the oppressive influence of circumstances crushing the individual soul. It is not society's fault that most men seem to miss their vocation. Most men have no vocation; and society, in imposing on them some chance language, some chance religion, and some chance career, first plants an ideal in their bosoms and insinuates into them a sort of racial or professional soul. Their only character is composed of the habits they have been led to acquire. Some little propensities betrayed in childhood may very probably survive; one man may prove by his dying words that he was congenitally witty,

Feeble individuality the rule.

another tender, another brave. But these native qualities will simply have added an ineffectual tint to some typical existence or other; and the vast majority will remain, as Schopenhauer said, *Fabrikwaaren der Natur.*

Variety in human dreams, like personality among savages, may indeed be inwardly very great, but it is not efficacious. To be socially important and expressible in some common medium, initial differences in temper must be organised into custom and become cumulative by being imitated and enforced. The only artists who can show great originality are those trained in distinct and established schools; for originality and genius must be largely fed and raised on the shoulders of some old tradition. A rich organisation and heritage, while they predetermine the core of all possible variations, increase their number, since every advance opens up new vistas; and growth, in extending the periphery of the substance organised, multiplies the number of points at which new growths may begin. Thus it is only in recent times that discoveries in science have been frequent, because natural science until lately possessed no settled method and no considerable fund of acquired truths. So, too, in political society, statesmanship is made possible by traditional policies, generalship by military institutions, great financiers by established commerce.

If we ventured to generalise these observations we might say that such an unequal distribution

of capacity as might justify aristocracy should be
looked for only in civilised states. Savages are
born free and equal, but wherever a complex and
highly specialised environment limits the loose
freedom of those born into it, it also stimulates
their capacity. Under forced culture remarkable
growths will appear, bringing to light possibilities
in men which might, perhaps, not even have been
possibilities had they been left to themselves; for
mulberry leaves do not of themselves develop into
brocade. A certain personal idiosyncrasy must be
assumed at bottom, else cotton damask would be
as good as silk and all men having like opportunities would be equally great. This idiosyncrasy is brought out by social pressure, while in
a state of nature it might have betrayed itself
only in trivial and futile ways, as it does among
barbarians.

Distinction is thus in one sense artificial, since
it cannot become important or practical unless a
certain environment gives play to individual talent and preserves its originality; but distinction
nevertheless is perfectly real, and not merely im-
Sophistical   puted. In vain does the man in the
envy.   street declare that he, too, could have
been a king if he had been born in the purple;
for that potentiality does not belong to him as he
is, but only as he might have been, if *per impossi-
bile* he had not been himself. There is a strange
metaphysical illusion in imagining that a man
might change his parents, his body, his early en-

vironment, and yet retain his personality. In its higher faculties his personality is produced by his special relations. If Shakespeare had been born in Italy he might, if you will, have been a great poet, but Shakespeare he could never have been. Nor can it be called an injustice to all of us who are not Englishmen of Queen Elizabeth's time that Shakespeare had that advantage and was thereby enabled to exist.

The sense of injustice at unequal opportunities arises only when the two environments compared are really somewhat analogous, so that the illusion of a change of rôles without a change of characters may retain some colour. It was a just insight, for instance, in the Christian fable to make the first rebel against God the chief among the angels, the spirit occupying the position nearest to that which he tried to usurp. Lucifer's fallacy consisted in thinking natural inequality artificial. His perversity lay in rebelling against himself and rejecting the happiness proper to his nature. This was the maddest possible way of rebelling against his true creator; for it is our particular finitude that creates us and makes us be. No one, except in wilful fancy, would envy the peculiar advantages of a whale or an ant, of an Inca or a Grand Lama. An exchange of places with such remote beings would too evidently leave each creature the very same that it was before; for after a nominal exchange of places each office would remain filled and no trace of a change would be perceptible. But the penny that one man finds and another misses would not, had fortune been reversed, have transmuted each man into the other. So adventitious a circumstance seems easily transferable without undermining that personal distinction which it had come to embitter. Yet the incipient fallacy lurking even in such suppositions becomes obvious when we inquire whether so blind an accident, for instance, as sex is also adventitious and ideally transferable and whether Jack and Jill, remaining themselves, could have exchanged genders.

What extends these invidious comparisons beyond all tolerable bounds is the generic and vague nature proper to language and its terms. The first personal pronoun " I " is a concept so thoroughly universal that it can accompany any experience whatever, yet it is used to designate an individual who is really definable not by the formal selfhood which he shares with every other thinker, but by the special events that make up his life. Each man's memory embraces a certain field, and if the landscape open to his vision is sad and hateful he naturally wishes it to shift and become like that paradise in which, as he fancies, other men dwell. A legitimate rebellion against evil in his own experience becomes an unthinkable supposition about what his experience might have been had *he* enjoyed those other men's opportunities or even (so far can unreason wander) had *he* possessed their character. The wholly different creature, a replica of that envied ideal, which would have existed in that case would still have called itself " I "; and so, the dreamer imagines, that creature would have been himself in a different situation.

If a new birth could still be called by a man's own name, the reason would be that the concrete faculties now present in him are the basis for the ideal he throws out, and if these particular faculties came to fruition in a new being, he would call that being himself, inasmuch as it realised his ideal. The poorer the reality, therefore, the meaner and vaguer the ideal it is able to project. Man is so tied to his personal endowment (essential to him though an accident in the world) that even his uttermost ideal, into which he would fly out of himself and his finitude, can be nothing but the fulfilment of his own initial idiosyncrasies. Whatever other wills and other glories may exist in heaven lie not within his universe of aspiration. Even his most perversely metaphysical envy can begrudge to others only what he instinctively craves for himself.

Inequality is not a grievance; suffering is. It is not mere inequality, therefore, that can be a reproach to the aristocratic or theistic ideal. Could each person fulfil his own nature the most striking differences in endowment and fortune would trouble nobody's dreams. The true reproach to which aristocracy and theism are open is the thwarting of those unequal natures and the

consequent suffering imposed on them all. Injustice in this world is not something comparative; the wrong is deep, clear, and absolute in
each private fate. A bruised child wailing in the
street, his small world for the moment utterly
black and cruel before him, does not fetch his unhappiness from sophisticated comparisons or irrational envy; nor can any compensations and celestial harmonies supervening later ever expunge or
justify that moment's bitterness. The pain may
be whistled away and forgotten; the mind may be
rendered by it only a little harder, a little coarser,
a little more secretive and sullen and familiar
with unrightable wrong. But ignoring that pain
will not prevent its having existed; it must remain for ever to trouble God's omniscience and
be a part of that hell which the creation too truly
involves.

The same curse of suffering vitiates Agrippa's
ingenious parable and the joyful humility of
Dante's celestial friends, and renders both equally
irrelevant to human conditions. Nature may ar-
range her hierarchies as she chooses and make
her creatures instrumental to one another's life.
That interrelation is no injury to any part and
an added beauty in the whole. It would have been
a truly admirable arrangement to have enabled
every living being, in attaining its own end, to
make the attainments of the others' ends possible
to them also. An approach to such an equilibrium
has actually been reached in some respects by the

rough sifting of miscellaneous organisms until those that were compatible alone remained. But **Mutilation by crowding.** nature, in her haste to be fertile, wants to produce everything at once, and her distracted industry has brought about terrible confusion and waste and terrible injustice. She has been led to punish her ministers for the services they render and her favourites for the honours they receive. She has imposed suffering on her creatures together with life; she has defeated her own objects and vitiated her bounty by letting every good do harm and bring evil in its train to some unsuspecting creature.

This oppression is the moral stain that attaches to aristocracy and makes it truly unjust. Every privilege that imposes suffering involves a wrong. Not only does aristocracy lay on the world a tax in labour and privation that its own splendours, intellectual and worldly, may arise, but by so doing it infects intelligence and grandeur with inhumanity and renders corrupt and odious that pre-eminence which should have been divine. The lower classes, in submitting to the hardship and meanness of their lives—which, to be sure, might have been harder and meaner had no aristocracy existed—must upbraid their fellow-men for profiting by their ill fortune and therefore having an interest in perpetuating it. Instead of the brutal but innocent injustice of nature, what they suffer from is the sly injustice of men; and though the suffering be less—for the worst of men is human

—the injury is more sensible. The inclemencies and dangers men must endure in a savage state, in scourging them, would not have profited by that cruelty. But suffering has an added sting when it enables others to be exempt from care and to live like the gods in irresponsible ease; the inequality which would have been innocent and even beautiful in a happy world becomes, in a painful world, a bitter wrong, or at best a criminal beauty.

A hint to optimists. It would be a happy relief to the aristocrat's conscience, when he possesses one, could he learn from some yet bolder Descartes that common people were nothing but *bêtes-machines,* and that only a groundless prejudice had hitherto led us to suppose that life could exist where evidently nothing good could be attained by living. If all unfortunate people could be proved to be unconscious automata, what a brilliant justification that would be for the ways of both God and man! Philosophy would not lack arguments to support such an agreeable conclusion. Beginning with the axiom that whatever is is right, a metaphysician might adduce the truth that consciousness is something self-existent and indubitably real; therefore, he would contend, it must be self-justifying and indubitably good. And he might continue by saying that a slave's life was not its own excuse for being, nor were the labours of a million drudges otherwise justified than by the conveniences which they supplied their masters with. *Ergo,* those servile operations could come to consciousness only where they attained their end, and the world could contain nothing but perfect and universal happiness. A divine omniscience and joy, shared by finite minds in so far as they might attain perfection, would be the only life in existence, and the notion that such a thing as pain, sorrow, or hatred could exist at all would forthwith vanish like the hideous and ridiculous illusion that it was. This argument may be recommended to apologetic writers as no weaker than those they commonly rely on, and infinitely more consoling.

But so long as people remain on what such an
How aristocra- invaluable optimist might call the low
cies might do level of sensuous thought, and so long
good. as we imagine that we exist and suffer,
an aristocratic regimen can only be justified by radiating benefit and by proving that were less given to those above less would be attained by those beneath them. Such reversion of benefit might take a material form, as when, by commercial guidance and military protection, a greater net product is secured to labour, even after all needful taxes have been levied upon it to support greatness. An industrial and political oligarchy might defend itself on that ground. Or the return might take the less positive form of opportunity, as it does when an aristocratic society has a democratic government. Here the people neither accept guidance nor require protection; but the existence of a rich and irresponsible class offers

them an ideal, such as it is, in their ambitious
struggles. For they too may grow rich, exercise
financial ascendancy, educate their sons like gen-
tlemen, and launch their daughters into fashion-
able society. Finally, if the only aristocracy recognised were an aristocracy of achievement, and
if public rewards followed personal merit, the reversion to the people might take the form of participation by them in the ideal interests of eminent
men. Holiness, genius, and knowledge can rever-
berate through all society. The fruits of art and
science are in themselves cheap and not to be
monopolised or consumed in enjoyment. On the
contrary, their wider diffusion stimulates their
growth and makes their cultivation more intense
and successful. When an ideal interest is general
the share which falls to the private person is the
more apt to be efficacious. The saints have usually had companions, and artists and philosophers
have flourished in schools.

At the same time ideal goods cannot be assimilated without some training and leisure. Like
education and religion they are degraded by popu-
larity, and reduced from what the master intended
to what the people are able and willing to receive.
So pleasing an idea, then, as this of diffused ideal
possessions has little application in a society aris-
tocratically framed; for the greater eminence the
few attain the less able are the many to follow
them. Great thoughts require a great mind and
pure beauties a profound sensibility. To attempt

to give such things a wide currency is to be willing to denaturalise them in order to boast that they have been propagated. Culture is on the horns of this dilemma : if profound and noble it must remain rare, if common it must become mean. These alternatives can never be eluded until some purified and high-bred race succeeds the promiscuous bipeds that now blacken the planet.

Aristocracy, like everything else, has no practical force save that which mechanical causes endow it with. Its privileges are fruits of inevitable advantages. Its oppressions are simply new forms and vehicles for nature's primeval cruelty, while the benefits it may also confer are only further examples of her nice equilibrium and necessary harmony. For it lies in the essence of a mechanical world, where the interests of its products are concerned, to be fundamentally kind, since it has formed and on the whole maintains those products, and yet continually cruel, since it forms and maintains them blindly, without considering difficulties or probable failures. Now the most tyrannical government, like the best, is a natural product maintained by an equilibrium of natural forces. It is simply a new mode of mechanical energy to which the philosopher living under it must adjust himself as he would to the weather.

Man adds wrong to nature's injury. But when the vehicle of nature's inclemency is a heartless man, even if the harm done be less, it puts on a new and a moral aspect. The source of injury is then not only natural but criminal as well, and the result is a sense of wrong added to misfortune. It must needs be that offence come, but woe to him by whom the offence cometh. He justly arouses indignation and endures remorse.

Now civilisation cannot afford to entangle its ideals with the causes of remorse and of just indignation. In the first place nature in her slow and ponderous way levels her processes and rubs off her sharp edges by perpetual friction. Where there is maladjustment there is no permanent physical stability. Therefore the ideal of society can never involve the infliction of injury on anybody for any purpose. Such an ideal would propose for a goal something out of equilibrium, a society which even if established could not maintain itself; but an ideal life must not tend to destroy its ideal by abolishing its own existence. In the second place, it is impossible on moral grounds that injustice should subsist in the ideal. The ideal means the perfect, and a supposed ideal in which wrong still subsisted would be the denial of perfection. The ideal state and the ideal universe should be a family where all are not equal, but where all are happy. So that an aristocratic or theistic system in order to deserve respect must discard its sinister apologies for evil and clearly propose such an order of existences, one superposed upon the other, as should involve no suffering on any of its

Conditions of a just inequality.

levels. The services required of each must involve no injury to any; to perform them should be made the servant's spontaneous and specific ideal. The privileges the system bestows on some must involve no outrage on the rest, and must not be paid for by mutilating other lives or thwarting their natural potentialities. For the humble to give their labour would then be blessed in reality, and not merely by imputation, while for the great to receive those benefits would be blessed also, not in fact only but in justice.

CHAPTER V

DEMOCRACY

The word democracy may stand for a natural

Democracy as an end and as a means. social equality in the body politic or for a constitutional form of government in which power lies more or less directly in the people's hands. The former may be called social democracy and the latter democratic government. The two differ widely, both in origin and in moral principle. Genetically considered, social democracy is something primitive, unintended, proper to communities where there is general competence and no marked personal eminence. It is the democracy of Arcadia, Switzerland, and the American pioneers. Such a community might be said to have also a democratic government, for everything in it is naturally democratic. There will be no aristocracy, no prestige; but instead an intelligent readiness to lend a hand and to do in unison whatever is done, not so much under leaders as by a kind of conspiring instinct and contagious sympathy. In other words, there will be that most democratic of governments—no government at all. But when pressure of circumstances, danger, or in-

ward strife makes recognised and prolonged guidance necessary to a social democracy, the form

**Natural democ-
racy leads to
monarchy.**
its government takes is that of a rudimentary monarchy, established by
election or general consent. A natu-
ral leader presents himself and he is instinctively
obeyed. He may indeed be freely criticised and
will not be screened by any pomp or traditional
mystery; he will be easy to replace and every
citizen will feel himself radically his equal. Yet
such a state is at the beginnings of monarchy
and aristocracy, close to the stage depicted in
Homer, where pre-eminences are still obviously
natural, although already over-emphasised by the
force of custom and wealth, and by the fission
of society into divergent classes.

Political democracy, on the other hand, is a late

**Artificial
democracy is
an extension of
privilege.**
and artificial product. It arises by
a gradual extension of aristocratic
privileges, through rebellion against
abuses, and in answer to restlessness
on the people's part. Its principle is not the
absence of eminence, but the discovery that existing eminence is no longer genuine and representative. It is compatible with a very complex government, great empire, and an aristocratic society;
it may retain, as notably in England and in all
ancient republics, many vestiges of older and less
democratic institutions. For under democratic
governments the people have not created the
state; they merely control it. Their suspicions

and jealousies are quieted by assigning to them a
voice, perhaps only a veto, in the administration;
but the state administered is a prodigious self-
created historical engine. Popular votes never
established the family, private property, religious
practices, or international frontiers. Institutions,
ideals, and administrators may all be such as the
popular classes could never have produced; but
these products of natural aristocracy are suffered
to subsist so long as no very urgent protest is
raised against them. The people's liberty consists not in their original responsibility for what
exists—for they are guiltless of it—but merely in
the faculty they have acquired of abolishing any
detail that may distress or wound them, and of
imposing any new measure, which, seen against
the background of existing laws, may commend
itself from time to time to their instinct and
mind.

If we turn from origins to ideals, the contrast
Ideals and   between social and political democ-
expedients.   racy is no less marked. Social democracy is a general ethical ideal, looking to
human equality and brotherhood, and inconsistent, in its radical form, with such institutions as
the family and hereditary property. Democratic
government, on the contrary, is merely a means
to an end, an expedient for the better and
smoother government of certain states at certain
junctures. It involves no special ideals of life;
it is a question of policy, namely, whether the

general interest will be better served by granting all men (and perhaps all women) an equal voice in elections. For political democracy, arising in great and complex states, must necessarily be a government by deputy, and the questions actually submitted to the people can be only very large rough matters of general policy or of confidence in party leaders.

We may now add a few reflections about each kind of democracy, regarding democratic government chiefly in its origin and phases (for its function is that of all government) and social democracy chiefly as an ideal, since its origin is simply that of society itself.

The possibility of intelligent selfishness and the prevalence of a selfishness far from intelligent **Well-founded** unite to make men wary in intrust-
distrust of ing their interests to one another's
rulers. Yet
experts, if ra- keeping. If passion never overcame
tional, would prudence, and if private prudence al-
serve common
interests. ways counselled what was profitable also to others, no objection could arise to an aristocratic policy. For if we assume a certain variety in endowments and functions among men, it would evidently conduce to the general convenience that each man should exercise his powers uncontrolled by the public voice. The government, having facilities for information and ready resources, might be left to determine all matters of policy; for its members' private interests would coincide with those of the public, and

even if prejudices and irrational habits prevented them from pursuing their own advantage, they would surely not err more frequently or more egregiously in that respect than would the private individual, to whose ignorant fancy every decision would otherwise have to be referred.

Thus in monarchy every expedient is seized upon to render the king's and the country's interests coincident; public prosperity fills his treasury, the arts adorn his court, justice rendered confirms his authority. If reason were efficacious kings might well be left to govern alone. Theologians, under the same hypothesis, might be trusted to draw up creeds and codes of morals; and, in fact, everyone with a gift for management or creation might be authorised to execute his plans. It is in this way, perhaps, that some social animals manage their affairs, for they seem to co-operate without external control. That their instinctive system is far from perfect we may safely take for granted; but government, too, is not always adequate or wise. What spoils such a spontaneous harmony is that people neither understand their own interests nor have the constancy to pursue them systematically; and further, that their personal or animal interests may actually clash, in so far as they have not been harmonised by reason.

To rationalise an interest is simply to correlate it with every other interest which it at all affects. In proportion as rational interests predominate in a man and he esteems rational satisfactions above all others, it becomes impossible that he should injure another by his action, and unnecessary that he should sacrifice himself. But the worse and more brutal his nature is, and the less satisfaction he finds in justice, the more need he has to do violence to himself, lest he should be doing it to others. This is the reason why preaching, conscious effort, and even education are such feeble agencies for moral reform: only selection and right breeding could produce that genuine virtue which would not need to find goodness unpalatable nor to say, in expressing its own perversities, that a distaste for excellence is a condition of being good. But when a man is ill-begotten and foolish, and hates the means to his own happiness, he naturally is not well fitted to secure that of other people. Those who suffer by his folly are apt to think him malicious, whereas he is the first to suffer himself and knows that it was the force of circumstances and a certain pathetic helplessness in his own soul that led him into his errors.

These errors, when they are committed by a weak and passionate ruler, are not easily forgiven. **People jealous of eminence.** His subjects attribute to him an intelligence he probably lacks; they call him treacherous or cruel when he is very likely yielding to lazy habits and to insidious traditions.

They see in every calamity that befalls them a proof that his interests are radically hostile to theirs, whereas it is only his conduct that is so. Accordingly, in proportion to their alertness and self-sufficiency, they clamour for the right to govern themselves, and usually secure it. Democratic government is founded on the decay of representative eminence. It indicates that natural leaders are no longer trusted merely because they are rich, enterprising, learned, or old. Their spontaneous action would go awry. They must not be allowed to act without control. Men of talent may be needed and used in a democratic state; they may be occasionally *hired;* but they will be closely watched and directed by the people, who fear otherwise to suffer the penalty of foolishly intrusting their affairs to other men's hands.

A fool, says a Spanish proverb, knows more at home than a wise man at his neighbour's. So democratic instinct assumes that, unless all those concerned keep a vigilant eye on the course of public business and frequently pronounce on its conduct, they will before long awake to the fact that they have been ignored and enslaved. The implication is that each man is the best judge of his own interests and of the means to advance them; or at least that by making himself his own guide he can in the end gain the requisite insight and thus not only attain his practical aims, but also some political and intellectual dignity.

All just government pursues the general good; the choice between aristocratic and democratic forms touches only the means to that end. One arrangement may well be better fitted to one place and time, and another to another. Everything depends on the existence or non-existence of available practical eminence. The democratic theory It is repre- is clearly wrong if it imagines that sentative. eminence is not naturally representative. Eminence is synthetic and represents what it synthesises. An eminence not representative would not constitute excellence, but merely extravagance or notoriety. Excellence in anything, whether thought, action, or feeling, consists in nothing but representation, in standing for many diffuse constituents reduced to harmony, so that the wise moment is filled with an activity in which the upshot of the experience concerned is mirrored and regarded, an activity just to all extant interests and speaking in their total behalf. But anything approaching such true excellence is as rare as it is great, and a democratic society, naturally jealous of greatness, may be excused for not expecting true greatness and for not even understanding what it is. A government is not made representative or just by the mechanical expedient of electing its members by universal suffrage. It becomes representative only by embodying in its policy, whether by instinct or high intelligence, the people's conscious and unconscious interests.

Democratic theory seems to be right, however, **But subject to decay.** about the actual failure of theocracies, monarchies, and oligarchies to remain representative and to secure the general good. The true eminence which natural leaders may have possessed in the beginning usually declines into a conventional and baseless authority. The guiding powers which came to save and express humanity fatten in office and end by reversing their function. The government reverts to the primeval robber; the church stands in the way of all wisdom. Under such circumstances it is a happy thing if the people possess enough initiative to assert themselves and, after clearing the ground in a more or less summary fashion, allow some new organisation, more representative of actual interests, to replace the old encumbrances and tyrannies.

Ancient citizenship a privilege. In the heroic ages of Greece and Rome patriotism was stimulated in manifold ways. The city was a fatherland, a church, an army, and almost a family. It had its own school of art, its own dialect, its own feasts, its own fables. Every possible social interest was either embodied in the love of country or, like friendship and fame, closely associated with it. Patriotism could then be expected to sway every mind at all capable of moral enthusiasm. Furthermore, only the flower of the population were citizens. In rural districts the farmer might be a freeman; but he probably had slaves whose work he merely superintended. The meaner and more debasing offices, mining, seafaring, domestic service, and the more laborious part of all industries, were relegated to slaves. The citizens were a privileged class. Military discipline and the street life natural in Mediterranean countries, kept public events and public men always under everybody's eyes: the state was a bodily presence. Democracy, when it arose in such communities, was still aristocratic; it imposed few new duties upon the common citizens, while it diffused many privileges and exemptions among them.

The social democracy which is the ideal of many in modern times, on the other hand, excludes slavery, unites whole nations and even all mankind into a society of equals, and admits no local or racial privileges by which the sense of fellowship may be stimulated. Public spirit could not be sustained in such a community by exemptions, rivalries, or ambitions. No one, indeed, would be a slave, everyone would have an elementary education and a chance to demonstrate his capacity; but he would be probably condemned to those occupations which in ancient republics were assigned to slaves. At least at the opening of his career he would find himself on the lowest subsisting plane of humanity, and he would probably remain on it throughout his life. In other words, the citizens of a social democracy would be all labourers; for

Modern democracy industrial.

even those who rose to be leaders would, in a genuine democracy, rise from the ranks and belong in education and habits to the same class as all the others.

Under such circumstances the first virtue which a democratic society would have to possess would be enthusiastic diligence. The motives for work **Dangers to** which have hitherto prevailed in the **current civili-** world have been want, ambition, and **sation.** love of occupation: in a social democracy, after the first was eliminated, the last alone would remain efficacious. Love of occupation, although it occasionally accompanies and cheers every sort of labour, could never induce men originally to undertake arduous and uninteresting tasks, nor to persevere in them if by chance or waywardness such tasks had been once undertaken. Inclination can never be the general motive for the work now imposed on the masses. Before labour can be its own reward it must become less continuous, more varied, more responsive to individual temperament and capacity. Otherwise it would not cease to repress and warp human faculties.

A state composed exclusively of such workmen and peasants as make up the bulk of modern nations would be an utterly barbarous state. Every liberal tradition would perish in it; and the rational and historic essence of patriotism itself would be lost. The emotion of it, no doubt, would endure, for it is not generosity that the people lack. They possess every impulse; it is experience that they cannot gather, for in gathering it they would be constituting those higher organs that make up an aristocratic society. Civilisation has hitherto consisted in diffusion and dilution of habits arising in privileged centres. It has not sprung from the people; it has arisen in their midst by a variation from them, and it has afterward imposed itself on them from above. All its founders in antiquity passed for demi-gods or were at least inspired by an oracle or a nymph. The vital genius thus bursting forth and speaking with authority gained a certain ascendency in the world; it mitigated barbarism without removing it. This is one fault, among others, which current civilisation has; it is artificial. If social democracy could breed a new civilisation out of the people, this new civilisation would be profounder than ours and more pervasive. But it doubtless cannot. What we have rests on conquest and conversion, on leadership and imitation, on mastership and service. To abolish aristocracy, in the sense of social privilege and sanctified authority would be to cut off the source from which all culture has hitherto flowed.

Is current civilisation a good? Civilisation, however, although we are wont to speak the word with a certain unction, is a thing whose value may be questioned. One way of defending the democratic ideal is to deny that civilisation is a

good. In one sense, indeed, social democracy is
essentially a reversion to a more simple life, more
Arcadian and idyllic than that which aristocracy
has fostered. Equality is more easily attained in
a patriarchal age than in an age of concentrated
and intense activities. Possessions, ideal and material, may be fewer in a simple community, but
they are more easily shared and bind men together
in moral and imaginative bonds instead of divid-
ing them, as do all highly elaborate ways of living
or thinking. The necessaries of life can be enjoyed by a rural people, living in a sparsely settled country, and among these necessaries might
be counted not only bread and rags, which everyone comes by in some fashion even in our society,
but that communal religion, poetry, and fellowship which the civilised poor are so often without.
If social democracy should triumph and take this
direction it would begin by greatly diminishing
the amount of labour performed in the world.
All instruments of luxury, many instruments of
vain knowledge and art, would no longer be produced. We might see the means of communication, lately so marvellously developed, again
disused ; the hulks of great steamers rusting in
harbours, the railway bridges collapsing and the
tunnels choked ; while a rural population, with a
few necessary and perfected manufactures, would
spread over the land and abandon the great cities
to ruin, calling them seats of Babylonian servi-
tude and folly.

Such anticipations may seem fantastic, and of course there is no probability that a reaction against material progress should set in in the near future, since as yet the tide of commercialism and population continues everywhere to rise; but does any thoughtful man suppose that these tendencies will be eternal and that the present experiment in civilisation is the last the world will see?

If social democracy, however, refused to diminish labour and wealth and proposed rather to accelerate material progress and keep every furnace at full blast, it would come face to face with a serious problem. By whom would the product be enjoyed? By those who created it? What sort of pleasures, arts, and sciences would those grimy workmen have time and energy for after a day of hot and unremitting exertion? What sort of religion would fill their Sabbaths and their dreams? We see how they spend their leisure to-day, when a strong aristocratic tradition and the presence of a rich class still profoundly influence popular ideals. Imagine those aristocratic influences removed, and would any head be lifted above a dead level of infinite dulness and vulgarity? Would mankind be anything but a trivial, sensuous, superstitious, custom-ridden herd? There is no tyranny so hateful as a vulgar and anonymous tyranny. It is all-permeating, all-thwarting; it blasts every budding novelty and sprig of genius with its omnipresent and fierce stupidity. Such

Horrors of materialistic democracy.

a headless people has the mind of a worm and the
claws of a dragon. Anyone would be a hero who
should quell the monster. A foreign invader or
domestic despot would at least have steps to his
throne, possible standing-places for art and intelligence; his supercilious indifference would dis-
countenance the popular gods, and allow some
courageous hand at last to shatter them. Social
democracy at high pressure would leave no room
for liberty. The only freeman in it would be
one whose whole ideal was to be an average man.

Perhaps, however, social democracy might take
a more liberal form. It might allow
the benefits of civilisation to be integrated in eminent men, whose influ-
ence in turn should direct and temper the general
life. This would be timocracy—a government by
men of merit. The same abilities which raised
these men to eminence would enable them to
apprehend ideal things and to employ material
resources for the common advantage. They would
formulate religion, cultivate the arts and sciences,
provide for government and all public conveniences, and inspire patriotism by their discourse
and example. At the same time a new motive
would be added to common labour, I mean ambition. For there would be not only a possibility
of greater reward but a possibility of greater service. The competitive motive which socialism is
supposed to destroy would be restored in timocracy, and an incentive offered to excellence and

Timocracy or
socialistic
aristocracy.

industry. The country's resources would increase for the very reason that somebody might conceivably profit by them; and everyone would have at least an ideal interest in ministering to that complete life which he or his children, or whoever was most capable of appreciation, was actually to enjoy.

Such a timocracy (of which the Roman Church is a good example) would differ from the social aristocracy that now exists only by the removal of hereditary advantages. People would be born equal, but they would grow unequal, and the only equality subsisting would be equality of opportunity. If power remained in the people's hands, the government would be democratic; but a full development of timocracy would allow the proved leader to gain great ascendancy. The better security the law offered that the men at the top should be excellent, the less restraint would it need to put upon them when once in their places. Their eminence would indeed have been factitious and their station undeserved if they were not able to see and do what was requisite better than the community at large. An assembly has only the lights common to the majority of its members, far less, therefore, than its members have when added together and less even than the wiser part of them.

A timocracy would therefore seem to unite the advantages of all forms of government and to avoid their respective abuses. It would promote

freedom scientifically. It might be a monarchy,
if men existed fit to be kings; but they would
have to give signs of their fitness and their honours would probably not be hereditary. Like
aristocracy, it would display a great diversity of
institutions and superposed classes, a stimulating
variety in ways of living; it would be favourable
to art and science and to noble idiosyncrasies.
Among its activities the culminating and most
conspicuous ones would be liberal. Yet there
would be no isolation of the aristocratic body; its
blood would be drawn from the people, and only
its traditions from itself. Like social democracy,
finally, it would be just and open to every man,
but it would not depress humanity nor wish to
cast everybody in a common mould.

There are immense difficulties, however, in the
way of such a Utopia, some physical and others
moral. Timocracy would have to begin by uproot-
ing the individual from his present natural soil
and transplanting him to that in which his spirit
might flourish best. This proposed transfer is
what makes the system ideally excellent, since nature is a means only; but it makes it also almost
impossible to establish, since nature is the only
efficacious power. Timocracy can arise only in
the few fortunate cases where material and social
forces have driven men to that situation in which
their souls can profit most, and where they find
no influences more persuasive than those which
are most liberating. It is clear, for instance, that

timocracy would exclude the family or greatly weaken it. Soul and body would be wholly transferred to that medium where **The difficulty** lay the creature's spiritual affinities; **the same as in** his origins would be disregarded on **all Socialism.** principle, except where they might help to forecast his disposition. Life would become heartily civic, corporate, conventual; otherwise opportunities would not be equal in the beginning, nor culture and happiness perfect in the end, and identical. We have seen, however, what difficulties and dangers surround any revolution in that ideal direction.

Even less perfect polities, that leave more to chance, would require a moral transformation in mankind if they were to be truly successful.

A motive which now generates political democracy, impatience of sacrifice, must, in a good social democracy, be turned into its opposite. Men must be glad to labour unselfishly in the spirit of art or of religious service: for if they labour selfishly, the higher organs of the state would perish, since only a few can profit by them materially; while if they neglect their work, civilisation loses that intensive development which it was proposed to maintain. Each man would need to forget himself and not to chafe under his natural limitations. He must find his happiness in seeing his daily task grow under his hands; and when, in speculative moments, he lifts his eyes from his labour, he must find an ideal satisfaction in patriotism, in love for that complex society to which he is contributing an infinitesimal service. He must learn to be happy without wealth, fame, or power, and with no reward save his modest livelihood and an ideal participation in his country's greatness. It is a spirit hardly to be maintained without a close organisation and much training; and as military and religious timocracies have depended on discipline and a minute rule of life, so an industrial timocracy would have to depend on guilds and unions, which would make large inroads upon personal freedom.

The masses would have to be plebeian in position and patrician in feeling.   The question here suggests itself whether such a citizen, once having accepted his humble lot, would be in a different position from the plebeians in an aristocracy. The same subordination would be imposed upon him, only the ground assigned for his submission would be no longer self-interest and necessity, but patriotic duty. This patriotism would have to be of an exalted type. Its end would not be, as in industrial society, to secure the private interests of each citizen; its end would be the glory and perfection of the state as imagination or philosophy might conceive them. This glory and perfection would not be a benefit to anyone who was not in some degree a philosopher and a poet. They would seem, then, to be the special interests of an aristocracy, not indeed an aristocracy of wealth or power, but an aristocracy of noble minds. Those whose hearts could prize the state's ideal perfection would be those in whom its benefits would be integrated. And the common citizen would find in their existence, and in his own participation in their virtue, the sole justification for his loyalty.

Ideal patriotism is not secured when each man, although without natural eminence, pursues his private interests. What renders man an imaginative and moral being is that in society he gives new aims to his life which could not have existed in solitude: the aims of friendship, religion, science, and art. All these aims, in a well-knit state, are covered by the single passion of patriotism; and then a conception of one's country, its history and mission becomes the touchstone of every ideal impulse. Timocracy requires this kind of patriotism in everybody; so that if public duty is not to become a sacrifice imposed on the many for the sake of the few, as in aristocracy, the reason can only be that the many covet, appreciate, and appropriate their country's ideal glories, quite as much as the favoured class ever could in any aristocracy.

Organisation for ideal ends breeds fanaticism. Is this possible? What might happen if the human race were immensely improved and exalted there is as yet no saying; but experience has given no example of efficacious devotion to communal ideals except in small cities, held together by close military and religious bonds and having no important relations to anything external. Even this antique virtue was short-lived and sadly thwarted by private and party passion. Where public spirit has held best, as at Sparta or (to take a very different type of communal passion) among the Jesuits, it has been paid for by a notable lack of spontaneity and wisdom; such inhuman devotion to an arbitrary end has made these societies odious. We may say, therefore, that a zeal sufficient to destroy selfishness is, as men are now constituted, worse than selfishness itself. In pursuing prizes for themselves people benefit their fellows more than in pursuing such narrow and irrational ideals as alone seem to be powerful in the world. To ambition, to the love of wealth and honour, to love of a liberty which meant opportunity for experiment and adventure, we owe whatever benefits we have derived from Greece and Rome, from Italy and England. It is doubtful whether a society which offered no personal prizes would inspire effort; and it is still more doubtful whether that effort, if actually stimulated by education, would be beneficent. For an indoctrinated and collective virtue turns easily to fanaticism; it imposes irrational sacrifices prompted by some abstract principle or habit once, perhaps, useful; but that convention soon becomes superstitious and ceases to represent general human excellence.

Now it is in the spirit of social democracy to

Public spirit the life of democracy. offer no prizes. Office in it, being the reward of no great distinction, brings no great honour, and being meanly paid it brings no great profit, at least while honestly administered. All wealth in a true democracy would be the fruit of personal exertion and would come too late to be nobly enjoyed or to teach the art of liberal living. It would be either accumulated irrationally or given away outright. And if fortunes could not be transmitted or used to found a great family they would lose their chief imaginative charm. The pleasures a democratic society affords are vulgar and not even by an amiable illusion can they become an aim in life. A life of pleasure requires an aristocratic setting to make it interesting or really conceivable. Intellectual and artistic greatness does not need prizes, but it sorely needs sympathy and a propitious environment. Genius, like goodness (which can stand alone), would arise in a democratic society as frequently as elsewhere; but it might not be so well fed or so well assimilated. There would at least be no artificial and simulated merit; everybody would take his ease in his inn and sprawl unbuttoned without respect for any finer judgment or performance than that which he himself was inclined to. The only excellence subsisting would be spontaneous excellence, inwardly prompted, sure of itself, and inwardly rewarded. For such excellence to grow general mankind must be notably transformed. If a noble and civilised democracy is to subsist, the common citizen must be something of a saint and something of a hero. We see therefore how justly flattering and profound, and at the same time how ominous, was Montesquieu's saying that the principle of democracy is virtue.

CHAPTER VI

FREE SOCIETY

Primacy of nature over spirit. Natural society unites beings in time and space; it fixes affection on those creatures on which we depend and to which our action must be adapted. Natural society begins at home and radiates over the world, as more and more things become tributary to our personal being. In marriage and the family, in industry, government, and war, attention is riveted on temporal existences, on the fortunes of particular bodies, natural or corporate. There is then a primacy of nature over spirit in social life; and this primacy, in a certain sense, endures to the end, since all spirit must be the spirit of something, and reason could not exist or be conceived at all unless a material organism, personal or social, lay beneath to give thought an occasion and a point of view, and to give preference a direction. Things could not be near or far, worse or better, unless a definite life were taken as a standard, a life lodged somewhere in space and time. Reason is a principle of order appearing in a subject-matter which in its subsistence and quantity must be an irrational datum. Reason expresses purpose, purpose expresses impulse, and impulse expresses a natural body with self-equilibrating powers.

At the same time, natural growths may be called achievements only because, when formed, they support a joyful and liberal experience. Nature's works first acquire a meaning in the commentaries they provoke; mechanical processes have interesting climaxes only from the point of view of the life that expresses them, in which their ebb and flow grows impassioned and vehement. Nature's values are imputed to her retroactively by spirit, which in its material dependence has a logical and moral primacy of its own. In themselves events are perfectly mechanical, steady, and fluid, not stopping where we see a goal nor avoiding what we call failures. And so they would always have remained in crude experience, if no cumulative reflection, no art, and no science had come to dominate and foreshorten that equable flow of substance, arresting it ideally in behalf of some rational interest.

Thus it comes to pass that rational interests have a certain ascendancy in the world, as well as an absolute authority over it; for they arise where an organic equilibrium has naturally established itself. Such an equilibrium maintains itself by virtue of the same necessity that produced it; without arresting the flux or introducing any miracle, it sustains in being an ideal form. This form is what consciousness corresponds to and raises to actual existence; so that significant thoughts are something which nature necessarily lingers upon and seems to serve. The being to whom they come is the most widely based and synthetic of her creatures. The mind spreads and soars in proportion as the body feeds on the surrounding world. Noble ideas, although rare and difficult to attain, are not naturally fugitive.

Consciousness is not ideal merely in its highest phases; it is ideal through and through. On one level as much as on another, it celebrates an attained balance in nature, or grieves at its collapse; it prophesies and remembers, it loves and dreams. It sees even nature from the point of view of ideal interests, and measures the flux of things by ideal standards. It registers its own movement, like that of its objects, entirely in ideal terms, looking to fixed goals of its own imagining, and using nothing in the operation but concretions in discourse. Primary mathematical notions, for instance, are evidences of a successful reactive method attained in the organism and translated in consciousness into a stable grammar which has wide applicability and great persistence, so that it has come to be elaborated ideally into prodigious abstract systems of thought. Every experience of

All experience at bottom liberal.

victory, eloquence, or beauty is a momentary success of the same kind, and if repeated and sustained becomes a spiritual possession.
Society also breeds its ideal harmonies.
At first it establishes affections between
beings naturally conjoined in the world; later it
grows sensitive to free and spiritual affinities, to
oneness of mind and sympathetic purposes. These
ideal affinities, although grounded like the others
on material relations (for sympathy presupposes
communication), do not have those relations for
their theme but rest on them merely as on a pedes-
tal from which they look away to their own realm,
as music, while sustained by vibrating instruments, looks away from them to its own universe
of sound.

Social experi-
ence has its
ideality too.

Ideal society is a drama enacted exclusively in
the imagination. Its personages are all mythical,
beginning with that brave protagonist
who calls himself I and speaks all the
soliloquies. When most nearly material these personages are human souls—the ideal life of particular bodies—or floating mortal reputations—echoes
of those ideal lives in one another. From this
relative substantiality they fade into notions of
country, posterity, humanity, and the gods. These
figures all represent some circle of events or forces
in the real world; but such representation, besides
being mythical, is usually most inadequate. The
boundaries of that province which each spirit pre-
sides over are vaguely drawn, the spirit itself be-

The self an
ideal.

ing correspondingly indefinite. This ambiguity is most conspicuous, perhaps, in the most absorbing of the personages which a man constructs in this imaginative fashion—his idea of himself. " There is society where none intrudes ; " and for most men sympathy with their imaginary selves is a powerful and dominant emotion. True memory offers but a meagre and interrupted vista of past experience, yet even that picture is far too rich a term for mental discourse to bandy about; a name with a few physical and social connotations is what must represent the man to his own thinkings. Or rather it is no memory, however eviscerated, that fulfils that office. A man's notion of himself is a concretion in discourse for which his more constant somatic feelings, his ruling interests, and his social relations furnish most of the substance.

The more reflective and self-conscious a man is the more completely will his experience be subsumed and absorbed in his perennial " I." If philosophy has come to reinforce this reflective egotism, he may even regard all nature as nothing but his half-voluntary dream and encourage himself thereby to give even to the physical world a dramatic and sentimental colour. But the more successful he is in stuffing everything into his self-consciousness, the more desolate will the void become which surrounds him. For self is, after all, but one term in a primitive dichotomy and would lose its specific and intimate character were it no longer

Romantic egotism.

contrasted with anything else. The egotist must therefore people the desert he has spread about him, and he naturally peoples it with mythical counterparts of himself. Sometimes, if his imagination is sensuous, his alter-egos are incarnate in the landscape, and he creates a poetic mythology; sometimes, when the inner life predominates, they are projected into his own forgotten past or infinite future. He will then say that all experience is really his own and that some inexplicable illusion has momentarily raised opaque partitions in his omniscient mind.

Philosophers less pretentious and more worldly than these have sometimes felt, in their way, the absorbing force of self-consciousness. La Rochefoucauld could describe *amour propre* as the spring of all human sentiments. *Amour propre* involves preoccupation not merely with the idea of self, but with that idea reproduced in other men's minds; the soliloquy has become a dialogue, or rather a solo with an echoing chorus. Interest in one's own social figure is to some extent a material interest, for other men's love or aversion is a principle read into their acts; and a social animal like man is dependent on other men's acts for his happiness. An individual's concern for the attitude society takes toward him is therefore in the first instance concern for his own practical welfare. But imagination here refines upon worldly interest. What others think of us would be of little moment did

Vanity.

it not, when known, so deeply tinge what we think of ourselves. Nothing could better prove the mythical character of self-consciousness than this extreme sensitiveness to alien opinions; for if a man really knew himself he would utterly despise the ignorant notions others might form on a subject in which he had such matchless opportunities for observation. Indeed, those opinions would hardly seem to him directed upon the reality at all, and he would laugh at them as he might at the stock fortune-telling of some itinerant gypsy.

As it is, however, the least breath of irresponsible and anonymous censure lashes our self-esteem and sometimes quite transforms our plans and affections. The passions grafted on wounded pride are the most inveterate; they are green and vigorous in old age. We crave support in vanity, as we do in religion, and never forgive contradictions in that sphere; for however persistent and passionate such prejudices may be, we know too well that they are woven of thin air. A hostile word, by starting a contrary imaginative current, buffets them rudely and threatens to dissolve their being.

The highest form of vanity is love of fame. It **Ambiguities of fame.** is a passion easy to deride but hard to understand, and in men who live at all by imagination almost impossible to eradicate. The good opinion of posterity can have no possible effect on our fortunes, and the practical value which reputation may temporarily have is quite absent in posthumous fame. The direct ob-

ject of this passion—that a name should survive
in men's mouths to which no adequate idea of its
original can be attached—seems a thin and fantastic satisfaction, especially when we consider
how little we should probably sympathise with the
creatures that are to remember us. What comfort
would it be to Virgil that boys still read him at
school, or to Pindar that he is sometimes men-
tioned in a world from which everything he loved
has departed? Yet, beneath this desire for nominal longevity, apparently so inane, there may lurk
an ideal ambition of which the ancients cannot
have been unconscious when they set so high a
value on fame. They often identified fame with
immortality, a subject on which they had far
more rational sentiments than have since prevailed.

Fame, as a noble mind conceives and desires
it, is not embodied in a monument, a biography,
or the repetition of a strange name by strangers;
it consists in the immortality of a man's work,
his spirit, his efficacy, in the perpetual rejuvena-
tion of his soul in the world. When Horace—
no model of magnanimity—wrote his *exegi monu-
mentum,* he was not thinking that the pleasure
he would continue to give would remind people
of his trivial personality, which indeed he never
particularly celebrated and which had much better
lie buried with his bones. He was thinking, of
course, of that pleasure itself; thinking that the
delight, half lyric, half sarcastic, which those deli-

cate cameos had given him to carve would be per-
ennially renewed in all who retraced them. Nay,
perhaps we may not go too far in saying that
Its possible even that impersonal satisfaction **was**
ideality. not the deepest he felt; the deepest,
very likely, flowed from the immortality, not of
his monument, but of the subject and passion it
commemorated; that tenderness, I mean, and that
disillusion with mortal life which rendered his
verse immortal. He had expressed, and in expressing appropriated, some recurring human moods,
some mocking renunciations; and he knew that
his spirit was immortal, being linked and identified with that portion of the truth. He had
become a little spokesman of humanity, uttering
what all experience repeats more or less articu-
lately; and even if he should cease to be honoured in men's memories, he would continue to
be unwittingly honoured and justified in their
lives.

What we may conceive to have come in this way
even within a Horace's apprehension is undoubtedly what has attached many nobler souls to fame.
With an inversion of moral derivations which all
mythical expression involves we speak of fame as
the reward of genius, whereas in truth genius, the
imaginative dominion of experience, is its own
reward and fame is but a foolish image by which
its worth is symbolised. When the Virgin in the
Magnificat says, " Behold, from henceforth all
generations shall call me blessed," the psalmist

surely means to express a spiritual exaltation
exempt from vanity; he merely translates into a
rhetorical figure the fact that what had been first
revealed to Mary would also bless all generations.
That the Church should in consequence deem and
pronounce her blessed is an incident describing,
but not creating, the unanimity in their religious
joys.   Fame is thus the outward sign or recognition of an inward representative authority re-
siding in genius or good fortune, an authority in
which lies the whole worth of fame.   Those will
substantially remember and honour us who keep
our ideals, and we shall live on in those ages whose
experience we have anticipated.

Free society differs from that which is natural
and legal precisely in this, that it does not cultivate relations which in the last analysis are experi-
enced and material, but turns exclusively to una-
nimities in meanings, to collaborations in an ideal
world.   The basis of free society is of course natural, as we said, but free society has ideal goals.
Spirits cannot touch save by becoming unanimous.
At the same time public opinion, reputation, and
impersonal sympathy reinforce only very general
feelings, and reinforce them vaguely; and as the
inner play of sentiment becomes precise, it craves
more specific points of support or comparison.   It
is in creatures of our own species that we chiefly
scent the aroma of inward sympathy, because it
is they that are visibly moved on the same occasions as ourselves; and it is to those among our

fellow-men who share our special haunts and habits that we feel more precise affinities. Though
the ground for such feeling is animal contact and
contagion, its deliverance does not revert to those
natural accidents, but concerns a represented sympathy in represented souls. Friendship, springing
from accidental association, terminates in a consciousness of ideal and essential agreement.

Comradeship. Comradeship is a form of friendship still akin to general sociability
and gregariousness. When men are "in the
same boat together," when a common anxiety,
occupation, or sport unites them, they feel their
human kinship in an intensified form without
any greater personal affinity subsisting between
them. The same effect is produced by a common estrangement from the rest of society. For
this reason comradeship lasts no longer than
the circumstances that bring it about. Its constancy is proportionate to the monotony of people's lives and minds. There is a lasting bond
among schoolfellows because no one can become
a boy again and have a new set of playmates.
There is a persistent comradeship with one's
countrymen, especially abroad, because seldom is
a man pliable and polyglot enough to be at home
among foreigners, or really to understand them.
There is an inevitable comradeship with men of
the same breeding or profession, however bad these
may be, because habits soon monopolise the man.
Nevertheless a greater buoyancy, a longer youth,

a richer experience, would break down all these limits of fellowship. Such clingings to the familiar are three parts dread of the unfamiliar and want of resource in its presence, for one part in them of genuine loyalty. Plasticity loves new moulds because it can fill them, but for a man of sluggish mind and bad manners there is decidedly no place like home.

Though comradeship is an accidental bond, it External conditions of friendship. is the condition of ideal friendship, for the ideal, in all spheres, is nothing but the accidental confirming itself and generating its own standard. Men must meet to love, and many other accidents besides conjunction must conspire to make a true friendship possible. In order that friendship may fulfil the conditions even of comradeship, it is requisite that the friends have the same social status, so that they may live at ease together and have congenial tastes. They must further have enough community of occupation and gifts to give each an appreciation of the other's faculty; for qualities are not complementary unless they are qualities of the same substance. Nothing must be actual in either friend that is not potential in the other.

Identity in sex required, For this reason, among others, friends are generally of the same sex, for when men and women agree, it is only in their conclusions; their reasons are always different. So that while intellectual harmony between men and women is easily possible, its delightful and

magic quality lies precisely in the fact that it
does not arise from mutual understanding, but
is a conspiracy of alien essences and a kissing,
as it were, in the dark. As man's body differs from woman's in sex and strength, so his
mind differs from hers in quality and function:
they can co-operate but can never fuse. The
human race, in its intellectual life, is organised
like the bees: the masculine soul is a worker, sex-
ually atrophied, and essentially dedicated to impersonal and universal arts; the feminine is a
queen, infinitely fertile, omnipresent in its brooding industry, but passive and abounding in intuitions without method and passions without justice.
Friendship with a woman is therefore apt to be
more or less than friendship: less, because there is
no intellectual parity; more, because (even when
the relation remains wholly dispassionate, as in
respect to old ladies) there is something mysterious and oracular about a woman's mind which
inspires a certain instinctive deference and puts
it out of the question to judge what she says by
masculine standards. She has a kind of sibylline
intuition and the right to be irrationally *à propos*.
There is a gallantry of the mind which pervades
all conversation with a lady, as there is a natural courtesy toward children and mystics; but
such a habit of respectful concession, marking as
it does an intellectual alienation as profound as
that which separates us from the dumb animals,
is radically incompatible with friendship.

Friends, moreover, should have been
and in age. young together. Much difference in age
defeats equality and forbids frankness on many
a fundamental subject; it confronts two minds of
unlike focus: one near-sighted and without perspective, the other seeng only the background of
present things. While comparisons in these respects may be interesting and borrowings sometimes possible, lending the older mind life and
the younger mind wisdom, such intercourse has
hardly the value of spontaneous sympathy, in
which the spark of mutual intelligence flies, as it
should, almost without words. Contagion is the
only source of valid mind-reading: you must imitate to understand, and where the plasticity of
two minds is not similar their mutual interpreta-
tions are necessarily false. They idealise in their
friends whatever they do not invent or ignore,
and the friendship which should have lived on
energies conspiring spontaneously together dies
into conscious appreciation.

All these are merely permissive conditions for
Constituents friendship; its positive essence is yet
of friendship. to find. How, we may ask, does the
vision of the general *socius,* humanity, become specific in the vision of a particular friend without
losing its ideality or reverting to practical values?
Of course, individuals might be singled out for
the special benefits they may have conferred; but
a friend's only gift is himself, and friendship is
not friendship, it is not a form of free or liberal

society, if it does not terminate in an ideal possession, in an object loved for its own sake. Such objects can be ideas only, not forces, for forces are subterranean and instrumental things, having only such value as they borrow from their ulterior effects and manifestations. To praise the utility of friendship, as the ancients so often did, and to regard it as a political institution justified, like victory or government, by its material results, is to lose one's moral bearings. The value of victory or good government is rather to be found in the fact that, among other things, it might render friendship possible. We are not to look now for what makes friendship useful, but for whatever may be found in friendship that may lend utility to life.

The first note that gives sociability a personal quality and raises the comrade into an incipient **Personal liking.** friend is doubtless sensuous affinity. Whatever reaction we may eventually make on an impression, after it has had time to soak in and to merge in some practical or intellectual habit, its first assault is always on the senses, and no sense is an indifferent organ. Each has, so to speak, its congenial rate of vibration and gives its stimuli a varying welcome. Little as we may attend to these instinctive hospitalities of sense, they betray themselves in unjustified likes and dislikes felt for casual persons and things, in the *je ne sais quoi* that makes instinctive sympathy. Voice, manner, aspect, hints of congenial

tastes and judgments, a jest in the right key, a
gesture marking the right aversions, all these
trifles leave behind a pervasive impression. We
reject a vision we find indigestible and without
congruity to our inner dream; we accept and in-
corporate another into our private pantheon, where
it becomes a legitimate figure, however dumb and
subsidiary it may remain.

In a refined nature these sensuous premonitions
of sympathy are seldom misleading. Liking cannot, of course, grow into friendship over night as
it might into love; the pleasing impression, even
if retained, will lie perfectly passive and harmless in the mind, until new and different impres-
sions follow to deepen the interest at first evoked
and to remove its centre of gravity altogether from
the senses. In love, if the field is clear, a single
glimpse may, like Tristan's potion, produce a violent and irresistible passion; but in friendship
the result remains more proportionate to the incidental causes, discrimination is preserved, jealousy and exclusiveness are avoided. That vigilant,
besetting, insatiable affection, so full of doubts
and torments, with which the lover follows his
object, is out of place here; for the friend has no
property in his friend's body or leisure or residual
ties; he accepts what is offered and what is acceptable, and the rest he leaves in peace. He is distinctly not his brother's keeper, for the society
of friends is free.

Friendship may indeed come to exist without

sensuous liking or comradeship to pave the way;
but unless intellectual sympathy and
moral appreciation are powerful
enough to react on natural instinct
and to produce in the end the personal affection
which at first was wanting, friendship does not
arise. Recognition given to a man's talent or
virtue is not properly friendship. Friends must
desire to live as much as possible together and to
share their work, thoughts, and pleasures. Good-
fellowship and sensuous affinity are indispensable
to give spiritual communion a personal accent;
otherwise men would be indifferent vehicles for
such thoughts and powers as emanated from them,
and attention would not be in any way arrested
or refracted by the human medium through which
it beheld the good.

The refracting human medium for ideas.

No natural vehicle, however, is indifferent; no natural organ is or
should be transparent. Transparency
is a virtue only in artificial instruments, organs
in which no blood flows and whose intrinsic operation is not itself a portion of human life. In
looking through a field-glass I do not wish to perceive the lenses nor to see rainbows about their
rim; yet I should not wish the eye itself to lose
its pigments and add no dyes to the bulks it dis-
cerns. The sense for colour is a vital endowment
and an ingredient in human happiness; but no
vitality is added by the intervention of further
media which are not themselves living organs.

Affection based on the refrac- tion.

A man is sometimes a coloured and sometimes a clear medium for the energies he exerts. When a thought conveyed or a work done enters alone into the observer's experience, no friendship is possible. This is always the case when the master is dead; for if his reconstructed personality retains any charm, it is only as an explanation or conceived nexus for the work he performed. In a philosopher or artist, too, personality is merely instrumental, for, although in a sense pervasive, a creative personality evaporates into its expression, and whatever part of it may not have been translated into ideas is completely negligible from the public point of view. That portion of a man's soul which he has not alienated and objectified is open only to those who know him otherwise than by his works and do not estimate him by his public attributions. Such persons are his friends. Into their lives he has entered not merely through an idea with which his name may be associated, nor through the fame of some feat he may have performed, but by awakening an inexpressible animal sympathy, by the contagion of emotions felt before the same objects. Estimation has been partly arrested at its medium and personal relations have added their homely accent to universal discourse. Friendship might thus be called ideal sympathy refracted by a human medium, or comradeship and sensuous affinity colouring a spiritual light.

If we approach friendship from above and compare it with more ideal loyalties, its characteristic is its animal warmth and its basis in chance

The medium must also be transparent. conjunctions; if we approach it from below and contrast it with mere comradeship or liking, its essence seems to be the presence of common ideal interests. That is a silly and effeminate friendship in which the parties are always thinking of the friendship itself and of how each stands in the other's eyes; a sentimental fancy of that sort, in which nothing tangible or ulterior brings people together, is rather a feeble form of love than properly a friendship. In extreme youth such a weakness may perhaps indicate capacity for friendship of a nobler type, because when taste and knowledge have not yet taken shape, the only way, often, in which ideal interests can herald themselves is in the guise of some imagined union from which it is vaguely felt they might be developed, just as in love sexual and social instincts mask themselves in an unreasoning obsession, or as for mystic devotion every ideal masks itself in God. All these sentimental feelings are at any rate mere preludes, but preludes in fortunate cases to more discriminating and solid interests, which such a tremulous overture may possibly pitch on a higher key.

The necessity of backing personal attachment with ideal interests is what makes true

Common interests indispensable. friendship so rare. It is found chiefly in youth, for youth best unites the two requisite conditions—affectionate comradeship and ardour in pursuing such liberal aims as may be pursued in common. Life in camp or college is favourable to friendship, for there generous activities are carried on in unison and yet leave leisure for playful expansion and opportunity for a choice in friends. The ancients, so long as they were free, spent their whole life in forum and palæstra, camp, theatre, and temple, and in consequence could live by friendship even in their maturer years; but modern life is unfavourable to its continuance. What with business cares, with political bonds remote and invisible, with the prior claims of family, and with individualities both of mind and habit growing daily more erratic, early friends find themselves very soon parted by unbridgeable chasms. For friendship to flourish personal life would have to become more public and social life more simple and humane.

Friendship between man and wife.   The tie that in contemporary society most nearly resembles the ancient ideal of friendship is a well-assorted marriage. In spite of intellectual disparity and of divergence in occupation, man and wife are bound together by a common dwelling, common friends, common affection for children, and, what is of great importance, common financial interests. These bonds often suffice for substantial and lasting unanimity, even when no ideal passion preceded; so that what is called a marriage of reason, if it is truly reasonable, may give a fair promise of happiness, since a normal married life can produce the sympathies it requires.

When the common ideal interests needed to give
friendship a noble strain become altogether pre-
dominant, so that comradeship and personal liking
may be dispensed with, friendship passes into
more and more political fellowships. Discipleship
is a union of this kind. Without claiming any
share in the master's private life, perhaps without having ever seen him, we
may enjoy communion with his mind
and feel his support and guidance in following
the ideal which links us together. Hero-worship
is an imaginative passion in which latent ideals
assume picturesque shapes and take actual persons
for their symbols. Such companionship, perhaps
wholly imaginary, is a very clear and simple example of ideal society. The unconscious hero, to
be sure, happens to exist, but his existence is irrelevant to his function, provided only he be present
to the idealising mind. There is or need be no
comradeship, no actual force or influence transmitted from him. Certain capacities and tendencies in the worshipper are brought to a focus by
the hero's image, who is thereby first discovered
and deputed to be a hero. He is an unmoved
mover, like Aristotle's God and like every ideal to
which thought or action is directed.

The symbol, however, is ambiguous in hero-
worship, being in one sense ideal, the representation of an inner demand, and in another sense
a sensible experience, the representative of an
external reality. Accordingly the symbol, when

Between mas-
ter and disci-
ple.

highly prized and long contemplated, may easily become an idol; that in it which is not ideal nor representative of the worshipper's demand may be imported confusedly into the total adored, and may thus receive a senseless worship. The devotion which was, in its origin, an ideal tendency grown conscious and expressed in fancy may thus become a mechanical force vitiating that ideal. For this reason it is very important that the first objects to fix the soul's admiration should be really admirable, for otherwise their accidental blemishes will corrupt the mind to which they appear *sub specie boni.*

Discipleship and hero-worship are

**Conflict be-
tween ideal
and natural
allegiance.**
not stable relations. Since the meaning they embody is ideal and radiates from within outward, and since the image to which that meaning is attributed is controlled by a real external object, meaning and image, as time goes on, will necessarily fall apart. The idol will be discredited. An ideal, ideally conceived and known to be an ideal, a spirit worshipped in spirit and in truth, will take the place of the pleasing phenomenon; and in regard to every actual being, however noble, discipleship will yield to emulation, and worship to an admiration more or less selective and critical.

A disembodied ideal, however, is unmanageable and vague; it cannot exercise the natural and material suasion proper to a model we are expected to imitate. The more fruitful procedure

is accordingly to idealise some historical figure
or natural force, to ignore or minimise in it what

Automatic idealisation of heroes. does not seem acceptable, and to retain at the same time all the unob-
jectionable personal colour and all the
graphic traits that can help to give that model
a persuasive vitality. This poetic process is all
the more successful for being automatic. It is in
this way that heroes and gods have been created.
A legend or fable lying in the mind and continually repeated gained insensibly at each recur-
rence some new eloquence, some fresh congruity
with the emotion it had already awakened, and
was destined to awake again. To measure the importance of this truth the reader need only conceive the distance traversed from the Achilles
that may have existed to the hero in Homer, or
from Jesus as he might have been in real life, or
even as he is in the gospels, to Christ in the
Church.

CHAPTER VII

PATRIOTISM

The creative social environment, since it eludes sense, must be represented symbolically. The mythical social idea most potent over practical minds is perhaps the idea of country. When a tribe, enlarged and domiciled, has become a state, much social feeling that was before evoked by things visible loses its sensuous object. Yet each man remains no less dependent than formerly on his nation, although less swayed by its visible presence and example; he is no less concerned, materially and ideally, in the fortunes of the community. If a sense for social relations is to endure, some symbol must take the place of the moving crowd, the visible stronghold, and the outspread fields and orchards that once made up his country; some intellectual figment must arise to focus political interests, no longer confined to the crops and the priest's medicinal auguries. It is altogether impossible that the individual should have a discursive and adequate knowledge of statecraft and economy. Whatever idea, then, he frames to represent his undistinguished political relations becomes the centre of his patriotism.

160

When intelligence is not keen this idea may remain sensuous. The visible instruments of social
life—chieftains, armies, monuments, the dialect
and dress of the district, with all customs and
pleasures traditional there—these are what a
sensuous man may understand by his country.
Bereft of these sensations he would feel lost and
incapable; the habits formed in that environment
would be galled by any other. This fondness for
home, this dread of change and exile, is all the love
of country he knows. If by chance, without too
much added thought, he could rise to a certain
poetic sentiment, he might feel attachment also
to the landscape, to the memorable spots and aspects of his native land. These objects, which
rhetoric calls sacred, might really have a certain
sanctity for him; a wave of pious emotion might
run over him at the sight of them, a pang when
in absence they were recalled. These very things,
however, like the man who prizes them, are dependent on a much larger system; and if patriotism is to embrace ideally what really produces
human well-being it should extend over a wider
field and to less picturable objects.

Ambiguous
limits of a
native coun-
try, geographi-
cal and moral.
To define one's country is not so
simple a matter as it may seem. The
habitat of a man's youth, to which
actual associations may bind him, is
hardly his country until he has conceived the
political and historical forces that include that
habitat in their sphere of influence and have de-

termined its familiar institutions. Such forces
are numerous and their spheres include one another like concentric rings. France, for instance,
is an uncommonly distinct and self-conscious nation, with a long historic identity and a compact
territory. Yet what is the France a Frenchman
is to think of and love? Paris itself has various
quarters and moral climates, one of which may
well be loved while another is detested. The
provinces have customs, temperaments, political
ideals, and even languages of their own. Is
Alsace-Lorraine beyond the pale of French patriotism? And if not, why utterly exclude French-
speaking Switzerland, the Channel Islands, Bel-
gium, or Quebec? Or is a Frenchman rather to
love the colonies by way of compensation? Is
an Algerian Moor or a native of Tonquin his true
fellow-citizen? Is Tahiti a part of his " country"? The truth is, if we look at the heart of
the matter, a Protestant born in Paris is less a
Frenchman than is a Catholic born in Geneva.

If we pass from geography to institutions the
same vagueness exists. France to one man represents the Revolution, to another the Empire, to a
third the Church, and the vestiges of the *ancien
régime.* Furthermore, how far into the past is
patriotism to look? Is Charlemagne one of the
glories of French history? Is it Julius Cæsar or
Vicingetorix that is to warm the patriotic heart?
Want of reflection and a blind subservience to the
colours of the map has led some historians to call

Roman victories defeats suffered by their country,
even when that country is essentially so Roman,
for instance, as Spain. With as good reason
might a Sicilian or a Florentine chafe under the
Latin conquest, or an American blush at the invasion of his country by the Pilgrim Fathers.
Indeed, even geographically, the limits and the
very heart of a man's country are often ambiguous. Was Alexander's country Macedon or
Greece? Was General Lee's the United States or
Virginia? The ancients defined their country
from within outward; its heart was the city and
its limits those of that city's dominion or affinities. Moderns generally define their country
rather stupidly by its administrative frontiers;
and yet an Austrian would have some difficulty
in applying even this conventional criterion.

The object of patriotism is in truth something
ideal, a moral entity definable only by the ties
which a man's imagination and reason can at any
moment recognise. If he has insight and depth
of feeling he will perceive that what deserves his
loyalty is the entire civilisation to which he owes
his spiritual life and into which that life will presently flow back, with whatever new elements he
may have added. Patriotism accordingly has two aspects: it is partly sentiment, by which it looks back upon the
sources of culture, and partly policy, or allegiance
to those ideals which, being suggested by what has
already been attained, animate the better organs

Sentimental
and political
patriotism.

of society and demand further embodiment. To
love one's country, unless that love is quite blind
and lazy, must involve a distinction between the
country's actual condition and its inherent ideal;
and this distinction in turn involves a demand for
changes and for effort. Party allegiance is a true
form of patriotism. For a party, at least in its
intent, is an association of persons advocating the
same policy. Every thoughtful man must advocate some policy, and unless he has the misfortune
to stand quite alone in his conception of public
welfare he will seek to carry out that policy by
the aid of such other persons as advocate it also.

The earth and the race the first objects of rational loyalty. The springs of culture, which retrospective patriotism regards, go back
in the last instance to cosmic forces.
The necessity that marshals the stars
makes possible the world men live in, and is the
first general and law-giver to every nation. The
earth's geography, its inexorable climates with
their flora and fauna, make a play-ground for the
human will which should be well surveyed by any
statesman who wishes to judge and act, not fan-
tastically, but with reference to the real situation.
Geography is a most enlightening science. In
describing the habitat of man it largely explains
his history. Animal battles give the right and
only key to human conflicts, for the superadded
rational element in man is not partisan, but on
the contrary insinuates into his economy the novel
principle of justice and peace. As this leaven,

however, can mingle only with elements predis-
posed to receive it, the basis of reason itself, in
so far as it attains expression, must be sought in
the natural world. The fortunes of the human
family among the animals thus come to concern
reason and to be the background of progress.

Within humanity the next sphere of interest
for a patriot is the race from which he is descended, with its traditional languages and religions. Blood is the ground of character and
intelligence. The fruits of civilisation may, indeed, be transmitted from one race to another and
consequently a certain artificial homogeneity may
be secured amongst different nations; yet unless
continual intermarriage takes place each race will
soon recast and vitiate the common inheritance.
The fall of the Roman Empire offered such a
spectacle, when various types of barbarism, with
a more or less classic veneer, re-established themselves everywhere. Perhaps modern cosmopolitanism, if not maintained by commerce or by
permanent conquest, may break apart in the
same way and yield to local civilisations no less
diverse than Christendom and Islam.

Community of race is a far deeper
bond than community of language,
education, or government. Where one
political system dominates various
races it forces their common culture to be external
merely. This is perhaps the secret of that strange
recrudescence of national feeling, apart often

Race, when distinct, the greatest of distinctions.

from political divisions, which has closely followed the French Revolution and the industrial era. The more two different peoples grow alike in externals the more conscious and jealous they become of diversity in their souls; and where individuals are too insignificant to preserve any personality or distinction of their own, they flock together into little intentional societies and factious groups, in the hope of giving their imagination, in its extremity, some little food and comfort. Private nationalities and private religions are luxuries at such a time in considerable demand. The future may possibly see in the Occident that divorce between administrative and ideal groups which is familiar in the Orient; so that under no matter what government and with utter cosmopolitanism in industry and science, each race may guard its own poetry, religion, and manners. Such traditions, however, would always be survivals or revivals rather than genuine expressions of life, because mind must either represent nature and the conditions of action or else be content to persist precariously and without a function, like a sort of ghost.

Some races are obviously superior to others. A more thorough adjustment to the conditions of existence has given their spirit victory, scope, and a relative stability. It is therefore of the greatest importance not to obscure this superiority by intermarriage with inferior stock, and thus nullify the progress made by a painful evolution and a

prolonged sifting of souls. Reason protests as
much as instinct against any fusion, for instance,
of white and black peoples. Mixture is in itself
no evil if the two nations, being approximately
equal, but having complementary gifts, can modify
them without ultimate loss, and possibly to advantage. Indeed the so-called pure
"Pure"
races may be races, since their purity has gone with
morally sterile. isolation and inexperience, have borne
comparatively little spiritual fruit. Large contact and concentrated living bring out native
genius, but mixture with an inferior stock can
only tend to obliterate it. The Jews, the Greeks,
the Romans, the English were never so great as
when they confronted other nations, reacting
against them and at the same time, perhaps,
adopting their culture; but this greatness fails inwardly whenever contact leads to amalgamation.

There is something unmistakably illiberal, almost superstitious, in standing on race for its
own sake, as if origins and not results were of
moral value. It matters nothing what blood a
man has, if he has the right spirit; and if there
is some ground for identifying the two (since
monkeys, however educated, are monkeys still)
it is only when blood means character and capacity, and is tested by them, that it becomes important. Nor is it unjust to level the individual,
in his political and moral status, with the race
to which he belongs, if this race holds an approved
position. Individual gifts and good intentions

have little efficacy in the body politic if they neither express a great tradition nor can avail to found one; and this tradition, as religion shows, will falsify individual insights so soon as they are launched into the public medium. The common soul will destroy a noble genius in absorbing it, and therefore, to maintain progress, a general genius has to be invoked; and a general genius means an exceptional and distinct race.

Environment, education, fashion, may be all powerful while they last and may make it seem a prejudice to insist on race, turning its assumed efficacy into a sheer dogma, with fanatical impulses behind it; yet in practice the question will soon recur: What shall sustain that omnipotent fashion, education, or environment? Nothing is more treacherous than tradition, when insight and force are lacking to keep it warm. Under Roman dominion, the inhabitants of Sparta still submitted to the laws of Lycurgus and their life continued to be a sort of ritualistic shadow of the past. Those enfranchised helots thought they were maintaining a heroic state when, in fact, they were only turning its forms into a retrospective religion. The old race was practically extinct; ephors, gymnasia, and common meals could do nothing to revive it. The ways of the Roman world—a kindred promiscuous population—prevailed over that local ritual and rendered it perfunctory, because there were no longer any living souls to understand that

True nationality direction on a definite ideal.

a man might place his happiness in his country's
life and care nothing for Oriental luxury or Oriental superstition, things coming to flatter his personal lusts and make him useless and unhappy.

Institutions without men are as futile as men
without institutions. Before race can be a rational object for patriotism there must exist a
traditional genius, handed down by inheritance
or else by adoption, when the persons adopted can
really appreciate the mysteries they are initiated
into. Blood could be disregarded, if only the
political ideal remained constant and progress
was sustained, the laws being modified only to
preserve their spirit. A state lives in any case
by exchanging persons, and all spiritual life is
maintained by exchanging expressions. Life is a
circulation; it can digest whatever materials will
assume a form already determined ideally and
enable that form to come forth more clearly and
be determined in more particulars. Stagnant matter necessarily decays and in effect is false to the
spirit no less than a spirit that changes is false
to itself.

The spirit of a race is a mythical entity expressing the individual soul in its most
constant and profound instincts and
expanding it in the direction in which
correct representation is most easily
possible, in the direction of ancestors, kinsmen,
and descendants. In ancient cities, where patriotism was intense, it was expressed in a tribal

Country well
represented by
domestic and
civic religion.

and civic religion. The lares, the local gods, the deified heroes associated with them, were either ancestors idealised or ideals of manhood taking the form of patrons and supernatural protectors. Jupiter Capitolinus and the Spirit of Rome were a single object. To worship Jupiter in that Capitol was to dedicate oneself to the service of Rome. A foreigner could no more share that devotion than a neighbour could share the religion of the hearth without sharing by adoption the life of the family. Paganism was the least artificial of religions and the most poetical; its myths were comparatively transparent and what they expressed was comparatively real. In that religion patriotism and family duties could take imaginable forms, and those forms, apart from the inevitable tinge of superstition which surrounded them, did not materially vitiate the allegiance due to the actual forces on which human happiness depends.

What has driven patriotism, as commonly felt and conceived, so far from rational courses and has attached it to vapid objects has been the initial illegitimacy of all governments. Under such circumstances, patriotism is merely a passion for ascendency. Properly it animates the army, the government, the aristocracy; from those circles it can percolate, not perhaps without the help of some sophistry and intimidation, into the mass of the people, who

Misleading identification of country with government.

Sporting or belligerent patriotism.

are told that their government's fortunes are their own. Now the rabble has a great propensity to take sides, promptly and passionately, in any spectacular contest; the least feeling of affinity, the slightest emotional consonance, will turn the balance and divert in one direction sympathetic forces which, for every practical purpose, might just as well have rushed the other way. Most governments are in truth private societies pitted against one another in the international arena and giving meantime at home exhibitions of eloquence and more rarely of enterprise; but the people's passions are easily enlisted in such a game, of course on the side of their own government, just as each college or region backs its own athletes, even to the extent of paying their bills. Nations give the same kind of support to their fighting governments, and the sporting passions and illusions concerned are what, in the national game, is called patriotism.

Where parties and governments are bad, as they are in most ages and countries, it makes practically no difference to a community, apart from local ravages, whether its own army or the enemy's is victorious in war, nor does it really affect any man's welfare whether the party he happens to belong to is in office or not. These issues concern, in such cases, only the army itself, whose lives and fortunes are at stake, or the official classes, who lose their places when their leaders fall from power. The private citizen in any event continues in such countries to pay a maximum of taxes and to suffer, in all his private interests, a maximum of vexation and neglect. Nevertheless, because he has some son at the front, some cousin in the government, or some historical sentiment for the flag and the nominal essence of his country, the oppressed subject will glow like the rest with patriotic ardour, and will decry as dead to duty and honour anyone who points out how perverse is this helpless allegiance to a government representing no public interest.

Exclusive patriotism rational only when the government supported is universally beneficent.   In proportion as governments become good and begin to operate for the general welfare, patriotism itself becomes representative and an expression of reason; but just in the same measure does hostility to that government on the part of foreigners become groundless and perverse. A competitive patriotism involves ill-will toward all other states and a secret and constant desire to see them thrashed and subordinated. It follows that a good government, while it justifies this governmental patriotism in its subjects, disallows it in all other men. For a good government is an international benefit, and the prosperity and true greatness of any country is a boon sooner or later to the whole world; it may eclipse alien governments and draw away local populations or industries, but it necessarily benefits alien individuals in so far as it is allowed to affect them at all.

Animosity against a well-governed country is therefore madness. A rational patriotism would rather take the form of imitating and supporting that so-called foreign country, and even, if practicable, of fusing with it. The invidious and aggressive form of patriotism, though inspired generally only by local conceit, would nevertheless be really justified if such conceit happened to be well grounded. A dream of universal predominance visiting a truly virtuous and intelligent people would be an aspiration toward universal beneficence. For every man who is governed at all must be governed by others; the point is, that the others, in ruling him, shall help him to be himself and give scope to his congenial activities. When coerced in that direction he obeys a force which, in the best sense of the word, *represents* him, and consequently he is truly free; nor could he be ruled by a more native and rightful authority than by one that divines and satisfies his true necessities.

A man's nature is not, however, a quantity or quality fixed unalterably and *a priori*.

Accidents of birth and training affect the ideal. As breeding and selection improve a race, so every experience modifies the individual and offers a changed basis for future experience. The language, religion, education, and prejudices acquired in youth bias character and predetermine the directions in which development may go on. A child might possibly change his country; a man can only wish that he might change it. Therefore, among the true interests which a government should represent, nationality itself must be included.

Mechanical forces, we must not weary of repeating, do not come merely to vitiate the ideal; they come to create it. The historical background of life is a part of its substance and the ideal can never grow independently of its spreading roots. A sanctity hangs about the sources of our being, whether physical, social, or imaginative. The ancients who kissed the earth on returning to their native country expressed nobly and passionately what every man feels for those regions and those traditions whence the sap of his own life has been sucked in. There is a profound friendliness in whatever revives primordial habits, however they may have been overlaid with later sophistications. For this reason the homelier words of a mother tongue, the more familiar assurances of an ancestral religion, and the very savour of childhood's dishes, remain always a potent means to awaken emotion. Such ingrained influences, in their vague totality, make a man's true nationality. A government, in order to represent the general interests of its subjects, must move in sympathy with their habits and memories; it must respect their idiosyncrasy for the same reason that it protects their lives. If parting from a single object of love be, as it is, true dying, how much more would a shifting of all the affections be death to the soul.

They are conditions and may contribute something.

Tenderness to such creative influences is a mark
of profundity; it has the same relation to political
life that transcendentalism has to science and
morals; it shrinks back into radical facts, into
centres of vital radiation, and quickens the sense
for inner origins. Nationality is a natural force
and a constituent in character which should be
reckoned with and by no means be allowed to miss
They are not those fruits which it alone might bear;
ends. but, like the things it venerates, it is
only a starting-point for liberal life. Just as to
be always talking about transcendental points of
reference, primordial reality, and the self to which
everything appears, though at first it might pass
for spiritual insight, is in the end nothing but
pedantry and impotence, so to be always harping
on nationality is to convert what should be a recognition of natural conditions into a ridiculous
pride in one's own oddities. Nature has hidden
the roots of things, and though botany must now
and then dig them up for the sake of compre-
hension, their place is still under ground, if flow-
ers and fruits are to be expected. The private
loyalties which a man must have toward his own
people, grounding as they alone can his morality
and genius, need nevertheless to be seldom paraded.
Attention, when well directed, turns rather to
making immanent racial forces blossom out in
the common medium and express themselves in
ways consonant with practical reason and universal progress. A man's feet must be planted

in his country, but his eyes should survey the world.

What a statesman might well aim at would be to give the special sentiments and gifts of his countrymen such a turn that, while continuing all vital traditions, they might find less and less of what is human alien to their genius. Differences in nationality, founded on race and habitat, must always subsist; but what has been superadded artificially by ignorance and bigotry may be gradually abolished in view of universal relations better understood. There is a certain plane on which all races, if they reach it at all, must live in common, the plane of morals and science; which is not to say that even in those activities the mind betrays no racial accent. What is excluded from science and morals is not variety, but contradiction. Any community which had begun to cultivate the Life of Reason in those highest fields would tend to live rationally on all subordinate levels also; for with science and morality rationally applied the best possible use would be made of every local and historical accident. Where traditions had some virtue or necessity about them they would be preserved; where they were remediable prejudices they would be superseded.

The symbol for country may be a man and may become an idol.   At the birth of society instincts existed, needful to the animal and having a certain glorious impetuosity about them, which prompted common action and speech, and a public morality, and men were led to construct myths that might seem to justify this co-operation. Paternal authority could easily suggest one symbol for social loyalty: the chief, probably a venerable and imperious personage, could be called a father and obeyed as a natural master. His command might by convention be regarded as an expression of the common voice, just as the father's will is by nature the representative of his children's interests. Again, the members of each community were distinguished from their enemies by many a sign and custom; these signs and customs might also become a graphic symbol for the common life.

Both these cases suggest how easily a symbol takes the place of its object and becomes an idol. If the symbol happens to be a man there are natural human sentiments awakened by him; and whatever respect his character or gifts may inspire, whatever charm there may be in his person, whatever graciousness he may add to his official favours or commands, increase immensely his personal ascendency. A king has a great opportunity to make himself loved. This scope given to private inclination is what, to ordinary fancy, makes royalty enviable; few envy its impersonal power and historic weight. Yet if a king were nothing but a man surrounded by flatterers, who was cheered when he drove abroad, there would be little stability in monarchy. A king is really the state's hinge and centre of gravity, the point where all private and party ambitions meet and, in a

sense, are neutralised. It is not easy for factions
to overturn him, for every other force in the state
will instinctively support him against faction. His
elevation above everyone, the identity of his sober
interests with those of the state at large, is cal-
culated to make him the people's natural representative; his word has therefore a genuine authority, and his ascendency, not being invidious,
is able to secure internal peace, even when not en-
lightened enough to insure prosperity or to avoid
foreign wars. Accordingly, whenever a monarchy
is at all representative time has an irresistible
tendency to increase its prestige; the king is felt
to be the guardian as well as the symbol of all
public greatness.

Meantime a double dislocation is possible here:
patriotism may be wholly identified with personal
loyalty to the sovereign, while the sovereign himself, instead of making public interests his own,
may direct his policy so as to satisfy his private
passions. The first confusion leads to a conflict
between tradition and reason; the second to the
ruin of either the state or the monarchy. In a
word, a symbol needs to remain transparent and
to become adequate; failing in either respect, it
misses its function.

**Feudal repre-
sentation sen-
sitive but par-
tial.**
The feudal system offers perhaps
the best illustration of a patriotism
wholly submerged in loyalty. The
sense of mutual obligation and service
was very clear in this case; the vassal in swearing

fealty knew perfectly well what sort of a bargain he was striking. A feudal government, while it lasted, was accordingly highly responsive and responsible. If false to its calling, it could be readily disowned, for it is easy to break an oath and to make new military associations, especially where territorial units are small and their links accidental. But this personal, conscious, and jealous subordination of man to man constituted a government of insignificant scope. Military functions were alone considered and the rest was allowed to shift for itself. Feudalism could have been possible only in a barbarous age when the arts existed on sufferance and lived on by little tentative resurrections. The feudal lord was a genuine representative of a very small part of his vassal's interests. This slight bond sufficed, however, to give him a great prestige and to stimulate in him all the habits and virtues of a responsible master; so that in England, where vestiges of feudalism abound to this day, there is an aristocracy not merely titular.

Monarchical representation comprehensive but treacherous. A highly concentrated monarchy presents the exactly opposite phenomenon. Here subordination is involuntary and mutual responsibility largely unconscious. On the other hand, the scope of representation is very wide and the monarch may well embody the whole life of the nation. A great court, with officers of state and a standing army, is sensitive to nothing so much as to general ap-

pearances and general results. The invisible forces
of industry, morality, and personal ambition that
really sustain the state are not studied or foment-
ed by such a government; so that when these resources begin to fail, the ensuing catastrophes are
a mystery to everybody. The king and his ministers never cease wondering how they can be so
constantly unfortunate.

So long, however, as the nation's vital force is
unspent and taxes and soldiers are available in
plenty, a great monarchy tends to turn those resources to notable results. The arts and sciences
are encouraged by the patronage of men of breeding and affairs; they are disciplined into a certain
firmness and amplitude which artists and scholars,
if left to themselves, are commonly incapable of.
Life is refined; religion itself, unless fanaticism
be too hopelessly in the ascendant, is co-ordinated
with other public interests and compelled to serve
mankind; a liberal life is made possible; the
imagination is stimulated and set free by that
same brilliant concentration of all human energies
which defeats practical liberty. At the same time
luxury and all manner of conceits are part and
parcel of such a courtly civilisation, and its best
products are the first to be lost; so that very likely
the dumb forces of society—hunger, conscience,
and malice—will not do any great harm when they
destroy those treacherous institutions which, after
giving the spirit a momentary expression, had become an offence to both spirit and flesh. Observ-

ers at the time may lament the collapse of so
much elegance and greatness; but nature has no
memory and brushes away without a qualm her
card-castle of yesterday, if a new constructive impulse possesses her to-day.

**Impersonal
symbols no
advantage.**
Where no suitable persons are found
to embody the state's unity, other symbols have to be chosen. Besides the
gods and their temples, there are the laws which
may, as among the Jews and Mohammedans, become as much a fetich as any monarch, and one
more long-lived; or else some traditional policy
of revenge or conquest, or even the country's name
or flag, may serve this symbolic purpose. A trivial
emblem, which no thinking man can substitute
for the thing signified, is not so great an advantage as at first sight it might seem; for in the
first place men are often thoughtless and adore
words and symbols with a terrible earnestness;
while, on the other hand, an abstract token, because of its natural insipidity, can be made to
stand for anything; so that patriotism, when it
uses pompous words alone for its stimulus, is very
apt to be a cloak for private interests, which the
speaker may sincerely conceive to be the only
interests in question.

The essence of patriotism is thus annulled, for
patriotism does not consist in considering the
private and sordid interests of others as well as
one's own, by a kind of sympathy which is
merely vicarious or epidemic selfishness; patriot-

ism consists rather in being sensitive to a set
of interests which no one could have had if he
had lived in isolation, but which accrue to men
conscious of living in society, and in a society
having the scope and history of a nation. It was
the vice of liberalism to believe that
common interests covered nothing but
the sum of those objects which each
individual might pursue alone; where-
by science, religion, art, language, and
nationality itself would cease to be matters of
public concern and would appeal to the individual
merely as instruments. The welfare of a flock of
sheep is secured if each is well fed and watered,
but the welfare of a human society involves the
partial withdrawal of every member from such
pursuits to attend instead to memory and to ideal
possessions; these involve a certain conscious continuity and organisation in the state not necessary
for animal existence. It is not for man's interest
to live unless he can live in the spirit, because
his spiritual capacity, when unused, will lacerate
and derange even his physical life. The brutal
individualist falls into the same error into which
despots fall when they declare war out of personal
pique or tax the people to build themselves a pyra-
mid, not discerning their country's interests, which
they might have appropriated, from interests of
their own which no one else can share.

Democracies, too, are full of patriots of this
lordly stripe, men whose patriotism consists in joy

Marginal note: Patriotism not self-interest, save to the social man whose aims are ideal.

at their personal possessions and in desire to increase them. The resultant of general selfishness might conceivably be a general order; but though intelligent selfishness, if universal, might suffice for good government, it could not suffice for nationality. Patriotism is an imaginative passion, and imagination is ingenuous. The value of patriotism is not utilitarian, but ideal. It belongs to the free forms of society and ennobles a man not so much because it nerves him to work or to die, which the basest passions may also do, but because it associates him, in working or dying, with an immortal and friendly companion, the spirit of his race. This he received from his ancestors tempered by their achievements, and may transmit to posterity qualified by his own.

CHAPTER VIII

IDEAL SOCIETY

To many beings—to almost all that people the
The grega-
rious instinct
all social in-
stincts in sus-
pense.
earth and sky—each soul is not attached by any practical interest. Some
are too distant to be perceived; the
proximity of others passes unnoticed.
It is far from requisite, in pursuing safety, that
every strange animal be regarded as either a friend
or an enemy. Wanton hostilities would waste
ammunition and idle attachments would waste
time. Yet it often happens that some of these
beings, having something in common with creatures we are wont to notice, since we stand to them
in sexual, parental, or hostile relations, cannot
well go unobserved. Their presence fills us with
a vague general emotion, the arrested possibility
at once of sexual, of parental, and of hostile ac-
tions. This emotion is gregarious or imperson-
ally social. The flock it commonly regards may
be described as an aggregate in which parents and
children have been submerged, in which mates are
not yet selected, and enemies not yet descried.

Gregarious sentiment is passive, watchful, ex-
pectant, at once powerful and indistinct, troubled

and fascinated by things merely possible. It renders solitude terrible without making society particularly delightful. A dull feeling of familiarity and comfort is all we can reasonably attribute to uninterrupted trooping together. Yet banishment from an accustomed society is often unbearable. A creature separated from his group finds all his social instincts bereft of objects and of possible exercise; the sexual, if by chance the sexual be at the time active; the parental, with all its extensions; and the combative, with all its supports. He is helpless and idle, deprived of all resource and employment. Yet when restored to his tribe, he merely resumes a normal existence. All particular feats and opportunities are still to seek. Company is not occupation. Society is like the air, necessary to breathe but insufficient to live on.

Similar beings herding together in the same places are naturally subject to simultaneous reactions, and the sense of this common reaction makes possible the conception of many minds having a common experience. The elements of this experience they express to one another by signs. For when spontaneous reactions occur together in many animals, each, knowing well his own emotion, will inevitably take the perceived attitude and gesture of his fellows for its expression—for his own attitude and gesture he knows nothing of; and he will thus possess, without further instruction, the outward sign for his inner experience.

It gives rise to conscience or sympathy with the public voice.   It is easy to see how a moral world can grow out of these primary intuitions. Knowing, for instance, the expression of anger, a man may come to find anger directed against himself; together with physical fear in the presence of attack, he will feel the contagion of his enemy's passion, especially if his enemy be the whole group whose reactions he is wont to share, and something in him will strive to be angry together with the rest of the world. He will perfectly understand that indignation against himself which in fact he instinctively shares. This self-condemning emotion will be his sense of shame and his conscience. Words soon come to give definition to such a feeling, which without expression in language would have but little stability. For when a man is attracted to an act, even if it be condemned by others, he views it as delightful and eligible in itself; but when he is forced, by the conventional use of words, to attach to that act an opprobrious epithet, an epithet which he himself has always applied with scorn, he finds himself unable to suppress the emotion connoted by the word; he cannot defend his rebellious intuition against the tyranny of language; he is inwardly confused and divided against himself, and out of his own mouth convicted of wickedness.

A proof of the notable influence that language has on these emotions may be found in their transformations. The connivance of a very few persons

is sufficient to establish among them a new application of eulogistic terms; it will suffice to suppress all qualms in the pursuance of their common
impulse and to consecrate a new ideal of character.
It is accordingly no paradox that there should be
honour among thieves, kindness among harlots,
and probity among fanatics. They have not lost
their conscience; they have merely introduced a
flattering heresy into the conventional code, to
make room for the particular passion indulged in
their little world.

Guises of pu.. Sympathy with the general mind
lic opinion. may also take other forms. Public
opinion, in a vivacious and clear-headed community, may be felt to be the casual and irresponsible
thing which in truth it is. Homer, for instance,
has no more solemn vehicle for it than the indefinite and unaccountable τις. "So," he tells us,
" somebody or anybody said." In the Greek trage-
dians this unauthoritative entity was replaced by
the chorus, an assemblage of conventional persons,
incapable of any original perception, but possessing a fund of traditional lore, a just if somewhat
encumbered conscience, and the gift of song. This
chorus was therefore much like the Christian
Church and like that celestial choir of which the
church wishes to be the earthly echo. Like the
church, the tragic chorus had authority, because
it represented a wide, if ill-digested, experience;
and it had solemnity, because it spoke in archaic
tropes, emotional and obscure symbols of prehis-

toric conflicts. These sacramental forms retained
their power to move in spite of their little perti-
nence to living issues, partly on account of the
mystery which enshrouded their forgotten passion
and partly on account of the fantastic interpreta-
tions which that pregnant obscurity allowed.

Far more powerful, however, are those embodiments of the general conscience which religion
Oracles and furnishes in its first and spontaneous
revelations. phase, as when the Hebrew prophets
dared to cry, " So saith the Lord." Such faith in
one's own inspiration is a more pliable oracle than
tradition or a tragic chorus, and more responsive
to the needs and changes of the hour. Occidental
philosophers, in their less simple and less eloquent
manner, have often repeated that arrogant Hebraic
cry: they have told us in their systems what God
thinks about the world. Such pretensions would
be surprising did we not remind ourselves of the
obvious truth that what men attribute to God is
nothing but the ideal they value and grope for in
themselves, and that the commandments, mythically said to come from the Most High, flow in
fact from common reason and local experience.

If history did not enable us to trace this derivation, the ever-present practical standard for faith
would sufficiently indicate it; for no one would
accept as divine a revelation which he felt to be
immoral or found to be pernicious. And yet such
a deviation into the maleficent is always possible
when a code is uprooted from its rational soil and

transplanted into a realm of imagination, where it is subject to all sorts of arbitrary distortions. If the sexual instinct should attach us (as in its extensions and dislocations it sometimes does) to beings incapable of satisfying it or of uniting with us in propagating the race, we should, of course, study to correct that aberration so that our joys and desires might march in step with the possible progress of the world. In the same way, if the gregarious instinct should bring us into the imagined presence of companions that really did not exist, or on whose attitude and co-operation our successes in no way depended, we should try to lead back our sense of fellowship to its natural foundations and possible sanctions.

Society exists so far as does analogous existence and community of ends. We may, in refining the social instinct, find some fellowship in the clouds and in the stars, for these, though remote, are companions of our career. By poetic analogy we may include in the social world whatever helps or thwarts our development, and is auxiliary to the energies of the soul, even if that object be inanimate. Whatever spirit in the past or future, or in the remotest regions of the sky, shares our love and pursuit, say of mathematics or of music, or of any ideal object, becomes, if we can somehow divine his existence, a partner in our joys and sorrows, and a welcome friend.

Those ideal objects, however, for whose sake all revolutions in space and time may be followed with interest, are not themselves members of our society. The ideal to which all forces should

The ideal a measure for all existences and no existence itself. minister is itself no force or factor in its own realisation. Such a possible disposition of things is a mere idea, eternal and inert, a form life might possibly take on and the one our endeavours, if they were consistent, would wish to impose on it. This ideal itself, however, has often been expressed in some mythical figure or Utopia. So to express it is simply to indulge an innocent instinct for prophecy and metaphor; but unfortunately the very innocence of fancy may engage it all the more hopelessly in a tangle of bad dreams. If we once identify our Utopia or other ideal with the real forces that surround us, or with any one of them, we have fallen into an illusion from which we shall emerge only after bitter disappointments; and even when we have come out again into the open, we shall long carry with us the desolating sense of wasted opportunities and vitiated characters. For to have taken our purposes for our helpers is to have defeated the first and ignored the second; it is to have neglected rational labour and at the same time debauched social sense.

The religious extensions of society should therefore be carefully watched; for while sometimes, as with the Hebrew prophets, religion gives dramatic expression to actual social forces and helps to intensify moral feeling, it often, as in mystics of all

creeds and ages, deadens the consciousness of real
ties by feigning ties which are purely imaginary.
This self-deception is the more frequent because
there float before men who live in the spirit ideals
which they look to with the respect naturally rendered to whatever is true, beautiful, or good; and
the symbolic rendering of these ideals, which is
the rational function of religion, may be confused
with its superstitious or utilitarian part—with
exploiting occult forces to aid us in the work of
life.

Occult forces may indeed exist, and they may
even be so disposed that the ideal is served by their
agency; but the most notable embodiment of a
principle is not itself a principle, being only an
instance, and the most exact fulfilment of a law
is not a law, being simply an event. To discover
a law may meantime be the most interesting of
events, and the image or formula that expresses
a principle may be the most welcome of intellectual presences. These symbols, weighted with their
wide significance, may hold the mind and attract
its energies into their vortex; and human genius
is certainly not at its worst when employed in
framing a good myth or a good argument. The
lover of representation, be he thinker or dramatist,
moves by preference in an ideal society. His communion with the world is half a soliloquy, for
the personages in his dialogue are private symbols, and being symbols they stand for what is not
themselves; the language he imputes to them is

his own, though it is their ways that prompt him
to impute that language to them. Plastic images
of his own making and shifting are his sole means
of envisaging eternal principles and ultimate substances, things ideal and potential, which can never
become phenomenal in their own persons.

It is an inspiring thought, and a
true one, that in proportion as a man's
interests become humane and his ef-
forts rational, he appropriates and ex-
pands a common life, which reappears in all individuals who reach the same impersonal level ·of
ideas—a level which his own influence may help
them to maintain. Patriotism envisages this ideal
life in so far as it is locally coloured and grounded
in certain racial aptitudes and traditions; but the
community recognised in patriotism is imbedded
in a larger one embracing all living creatures.
While in some respects we find sympathy more
complete the nearer home we remain, in another
sense there is no true companionship except with
the universe. Instinctive society, with its compulsory affections, is of course deeper and more elementary than any free or intellectual union. Love
is at once more animal than friendship and more
divine; and the same thing may be said of family
affection when compared with patriotism. What
lies nearer the roots of our being must needs enjoy a wider prevalence and engage the soul more
completely, being able to touch its depths and hush
its primordial murmurs.

Contrast be-
tween natural
and intellectual
bonds.

On the other hand, the free spirit, the political and speculative genius in man, chafes under those blind involutions and material bonds. Natural, beneficent, sacred, as in a sense they may be, they somehow oppress the intellect and, like a brooding mother, half stifle what they feed. Something drives the youth afield, into solitude, into alien friendships; only in the face of nature and an indifferent world can he become himself. Such a flight from home and all its pieties grows more urgent when there is some real conflict of temper or conscience between the young man and what is established in his family; and this happens often because, after all, the most beneficent conventions are but mechanisms which must ignore the nicer sensibilities and divergences of living souls.

Common men accept these spiritual tyrannies, weak men repine at them, and great men break them down. But to defy the world is a serious business, and requires the greatest courage, even if the defiance touch in the first place only the world's ideals. Most men's conscience, habits, and opinions are borrowed from convention and gather continual comforting assurances from the same social consensus that originally suggested them. To reverse this process, to consult one's own experience and elicit one's own judgment, challenging those in vogue, seems too often audacious and futile; but there are impetuous minds born to disregard the chances against

Appeal from man to God, from real to ideal society.

them, even to the extent of denying that they are taking chances at all. For in the first instance it never occurs to the inventor that he is the source of his new insight; he thinks he has merely opened his eyes and seen what, by an inconceivable folly, the whole world had grown blind to. Wise men in antiquity, he imagines, saw the facts as he sees them, as the gods see them now, and as all sane men shall see them henceforward.

Thus, if the innovator be a religious soul, grown conscious of some new spiritual principle, he will try to find support for his inspiration in some lost book of the law or in some early divine revelation corrupted, as he will assert, by wicked men, or even in some direct voice from heaven; no delusion will be too obvious, no re-interpretation too forced, if it can help him to find external support somewhere for his spontaneous conviction. To denounce one authority he needs to invoke another, and if no other be found, he will invent or, as they say, he will postulate one. His courage in facing the actual world is thus supported by his ability to expand the world in imagination. In separating himself from his fellow-men he has made a new companion out of his ideal. An impetuous spirit when betrayed by the world will cry, " I know that my redeemer liveth "; and the antiphonal response will come more wistfully after reflection:

> " It fortifies my soul to know
> That though I wander, Truth is so."

The deceptions which nature practises on men
are not always cruel. These are also
kindly deceptions which prompt him
to pursue or expect his own good when,
though not destined to come in the
form he looks for, this good is really destined to
come in some shape or other. Such, for instance,
are the illusions of romantic love, which may
really terminate in a family life practically better
than the absolute and chimerical unions which
that love had dreamed of. Such, again, are those
illusions of conscience which attach unspeakable
vague penalties and repugnances to acts which
commonly have bad results, though these are impossible to forecast with precision. When disillusion comes, while it may bring a momentary
shock, it ends by producing a settled satisfaction
unknown before, a satisfaction which the coveted
prize, could it have been attained, would hardly
have secured. When on the day of judgment, or
earlier, a man perceives that what he thought he
was doing for the Lord's sake he was really doing
for the benefit of the least, perhaps, of the Lord's
creatures, his satisfaction, after a moment's sur-
prise, will certainly be very genuine.

Such kindly illusions are involved in the symbolic method by which general relations and the
inconceivably diffuse reality of things
have to be apprehended. The stars are
in human thought a symbol for the silent forces
of destiny, really embodied in forms beyond our

Significant symbols revert to the concrete.

Nature a symbol for destiny.

apprehension; for who shall say what actual being may or may not correspond to that potentiality of life or sensation which is all that the external world can be to our science? When astrology invented the horoscope it made an absurdly premature translation of celestial hieroglyphics into that language of universal destiny which in the end they may be made to speak. The perfect astronomer, when he understood at last exactly what pragmatic value the universe has, and what fortunes the stars actually forebode, would be pleasantly surprised to discover that he was nothing but an astrologer grown competent and honest.

Ideal society belongs entirely to this realm of kindly illusion, for it is the society of symbols. Whenever religion, art, or science presents us with an image or a formula, involving no matter how momentous a truth, there is something delusive in the representation. It needs translation into the detailed experience which it sums up in our own past or prophecies elsewhere. This eventual change in form, far from nullifying our knowledge, can alone legitimise it. A conception not reducible to the small change of daily experience is like a currency not exchangeable for articles of consumption; it is not a symbol, but a fraud.

Representative notions have also inherent values. And yet there is another aspect to the matter. Symbols are presences, and they are those particularly congenial presences which we have inwardly evoked and cast in a form intelligible and familiar to human thinking. Their function is to give flat experience a rational perspective, translating the general flux into stable objects and making it representable in human discourse. They are therefore precious, not only for their representative or practical value, implying useful adjustments to the environing world, but even more, sometimes, for their immediate or æsthetic power, for their kinship to the spirit they enlighten and exercise.

This is prevailingly true in the fine arts which seem to express man even more than they express nature; although in art also the symbol would lose all its significance and much of its inward articulation if natural objects and eventual experience could be disregarded in constructing it. In music, indeed, this ulterior significance is reduced to a minimum; yet it persists, since music brings an ideal object before the mind which needs, to some extent, translation into terms no longer musical —terms, for instance, of skill, dramatic passion, or moral sentiment. But in music pre-eminently, and very largely in all the arts, external propriety is adventitious; so much can the mere presence and weight of a symbol fill the mind and constitute an absolute possession.

In religion and science the overt purpose of symbols is to represent external truths. The inventors of these symbols think they are merely uncovering a self-existent reality, having in itself the very form seen in their idea. They do not per-

Religion and science indirectly cognitive and directly ideal.

ceive that the society of God or Nature is an ideal society, nor that these phantoms, looming in their imagination, are but significant figments whose existent basis is a minute and indefinite series of ordinary perceptions. They consequently attribute whatever value their genial syntheses may have to the object as they picture it. The gods have, they fancy, the aspect and passions, the history and influence which their myth unfolds; nature in its turn contains hypostatically just those laws and forces which are described by theory. Consequently the presence of God or Nature seems to the mythologist not an ideal, but a real and mutual society, as if collateral beings, endowed with the conceived characters, actually existed as men exist. But this opinion is untenable. As Hobbes said, in a phrase which ought to be inscribed in golden letters over the head of every talking philosopher: *No discourse whatsoever can end in absolute knowledge of fact.* Absolute knowledge of fact is immediate, it is experiential. We should have to *become* God or Nature in order to know for a fact that they existed. Intellectual knowledge, on the other hand, where it relates to existence, is faith only, a faith which in these matters means trust. For the forces of Nature or the gods, if they had crude existence, so that we might conceivably become what they are, would lose that causal and that religious function which are their essence respectively. They would be merely collateral existences, loaded with all sorts of irrelevant properties, parts of the universal flux, members of a natural society; and while as such they would have their relative importance, they would be embraced in turn within an intelligible system of relations, while their rights and dignities would need to be determined by some supervening ideal. A nature existing in act would require metaphysics—the account of a deeper nature—to express its relation to the mind that knew and judged it. Any actual god would need to possess a religion of his own, in order to fix his ideal of conduct and his rights in respect to his creatures or rather, as we should then be, to his neighbours. This situation may have no terrors for the thoughtless; but it evidently introduces something deeper than Nature and something higher than God, depriving these words of the best sense in which a philosopher might care to use them.

Their opposite outlook. The divine and the material are contrasted points of reference required by the actual. Reason, working on the immediate flux of appearances, reaches these ideal realms and, resting in them, perforce calls them realities. One—the realm of causes—supplies appearances with a basis and calculable order; the other—the realm of truth and felicity—supplies them with a standard and justification. Natural society may accordingly be contrasted with ideal society, not because Nature is not, logically speaking, ideal too, but because in natural society we ally ourselves consciously with our origins and surroundings, in ideal society with our purposes. There is an immense difference in spirituality, in ideality of the moral sort, between gathering or conciliating forces for action and fixing the ends which action should pursue. Both fields are ideal in the sense that intelligence alone could discover or exploit them; yet to call nature ideal is undoubtedly equivocal, since its ideal function is precisely to be the substance and cause of the given flux, a ground-work for experience which, while merely inferred and potential, is none the less mechanical and material. The ideality of nature is indeed of such a sort as to be forfeited if the trusty instrument and true antecedent of human life were not found there. We should be frivolous and inconstant, taking our philosophy for a game and not for method in living, if having set out to look for the causes and practical order of things, and having found them, we should declare that they were not *really* casual or efficient, on the strange ground that our discovery of them had been a feat of intelligence and had proved a priceless boon. The absurdity could not be greater if in moral science, after the goal of all effort had been determined and happiness defined, we declared that this was not *really* the good.

Those who are shocked at the assertion that God and Nature are ideal, and that their contrasted prerogatives depend on that fact, may, of course, use the same words in a different way, making

them synonymous, and may readily " prove " that
God or Nature exists materially and has absolute
being. We need but agree to designate by those
terms the sum of existences, whatever they (or it)
may be to their own feeling. Then the ontologi-
cal proof asserts its rights unmistakably. Science
and religion, however, are superfluous if what we
wish to learn is that there is Something, and that
All-there-is must assuredly be All-there-is. Ecsta-
sies may doubtless ensue upon considering that
Being is and Non-Being is not, as they are said to
ensue upon long enough considering one's navel;
but the Life of Reason is made of more variegated
stuff. Science, when it is not dialectical, describes
an ideal order of existences in space and time,
such that all incidental facts, as they come, may
fill it in and lend it body. Religion, when pure,
contemplates some pertinent ideal of intelligence
and goodness. Both religion and science live in
imaginative discourse, one being an aspiration and
the other a hypothesis. Both introduce into the
mind an ideal society.

The Life of Reason is no fair reproduction of
the universe, but the expression of man alone. A
theory of nature is nothing but a mass of observations, made with a hunter's and an artist's eye.
A mortal has no time for sympathy with his victim
or his model; and, beyond a certain range, he has
no capacity for such sympathy. As in order to live
he must devour one-half the world and disregard
the other, so in order to think and practically to

know he must deal summarily and selfishly with his materials; otherwise his intellect would melt again into endless and irrevocable dreams. The law of gravity, because it so notably unifies the motions of matter, is something which these motions themselves know nothing of; it is a description of them in terms of human discourse. Such discourse can never assure us absolutely that the motions it forecasts will occur; the sensible proof must ensue spontaneously in its own good time. In the interval our theory remains pure presumption and hypothesis. Reliable as it may be in that capacity, it is no replica of anything on its own level existing beyond. It creates, like all intelligence, a secondary and merely symbolic world.

When this diversity between the truest theory and the simplest fact, between potential generalities and actual particulars, has been thoroughly appreciated, it becomes clear that much of what is valued in science and religion is not lodged in the miscellany underlying these creations of reason, but is lodged rather in the rational activity itself, and in the intrinsic beauty of all symbols bred in a genial mind. Of course, if these symbols had no real points of reference, if they were symbols of nothing, they could have no great claim to consideration and no rational character; at most they would be agreeable sensations. They are, however, at their best good symbols for a diffused experience having a certain order and tendency; they render that reality with a difference, reducing it to a formula or a myth, in which its tortuous length and trivial detail can be surveyed to advantage without undue waste or fatigue. Symbols may thus become eloquent, vivid, important, being endowed with both poetic grandeur and practical truth.

The facts from which this truth is borrowed, if they were rehearsed unimaginatively, in their own flat infinity, would be far from arousing the same emotions. The human eye sees in perspective; its glory would vanish were it reduced to a crawling, exploring antenna. Not that it loves to falsify anything. That to the worm the landscape might possess no light and shade, that the mountain's atomic structure should be unpicturable, cannot distress the landscape gardener nor the poet; what concerns them is the effect such things may produce in the human fancy, so that the soul may live in a congenial world.

Naturalist and prophet are landscape painters on canvases of their own; each is interested in his own perception and perspective, which, if he takes the trouble to reflect, need not deceive him about what the world would be if not foreshortened in that particular manner. This special interpretation is nevertheless precious and shows up the world in that light in which it interests naturalists or prophets to see it. Their figments make their chosen world, as the painter's apperceptions are the breath of his nostrils.

While the symbol's applicability is essential to its worth—since otherwise science would be useless and religion demoralising—its power and fascination lie in its acquiring a more and more profound affinity to the human mind, so long as it can do so without surrendering its relevance to practice.

Science should be mathematical and religion anthropomorphic.

Thus natural science is at its best when it is most thoroughly mathematical, since what can be expressed mathematically can speak a human language. In such science only the ultimate material elements remain surds; all their further movement and complication can be represented in that kind of thought which is most intimately satisfactory and perspicuous. And in like manner, religion is at its best when it is most anthropomorphic; indeed, the two most spiritual religions, Buddhism and Christianity, have actually raised a man, overflowing with utterly human tenderness and pathos, to the place usually occupied only by cosmic and thundering deities. The human heart is lifted above misfortune and encouraged to pursue unswervingly its inmost ideal when no compromise is any longer attempted with what is not moral or human, and Prometheus is honestly proclaimed to be holier than Zeus. At that moment religion ceases to be superstitious and becomes a rational discipline, an effort to perfect the spirit rather than to intimidate it.

Summary of this book. We have seen that society has three stages—the natural, the free, and the ideal. In the natural stage its function is to produce the individual and equip him with the prerequisites of moral freedom. When this end is attained society can rise to friendship, to unanimity and disinterested sympathy, where the ground of association is some ideal interest, while this association constitutes at the same time a personal and emotional bond. Ideal society, on the contrary, transcends accidental conjunctions altogether. Here the ideal interests themselves take possession of the mind; its companions are the symbols it breeds and possesses for excellence, beauty, and truth. Religion, art, and science are the chief spheres in which ideal companionship is found. It remains for us to traverse these provinces in turn and see to what extent the Life of Reason may flourish there.

A CATALOGUE OF
SELECTED DOVER BOOKS
IN ALL FIELDS OF INTEREST

A CATALOGUE OF SELECTED DOVER
BOOKS IN ALL FIELDS OF INTEREST

CONDITIONED REFLEXES, Ivan P. Pavlov. Full translation of most complete statement of Pavlov's work; cerebral damage, conditioned reflex, experiments with dogs, sleep, similar topics of great importance. 430pp. 5⅜ x 8½.   60614-7 Pa. $4.50

NOTES ON NURSING: WHAT IT IS, AND WHAT IT IS NOT, Florence Nightingale. Outspoken writings by founder of modern nursing. When first published (1860) it played an important role in much needed revolution in nursing. Still stimulating. 140pp. 5⅜ x 8½.   22340-X Pa. $2.50

HARTER'S PICTURE ARCHIVE FOR COLLAGE AND ILLUSTRATION, Jim Harter. Over 300 authentic, rare 19th-century engravings selected by noted collagist for artists, designers, decoupeurs, etc. Machines, people, animals, etc., printed one side of page. 25 scene plates for backgrounds. 6 collages by Harter, Satty, Singer, Evans. Introduction. 192pp. 8⅞ x 11¾.   23659-5 Pa. $4.50

MANUAL OF TRADITIONAL WOOD CARVING, edited by Paul N. Hasluck. Possibly the best book in English on the craft of wood carving. Practical instructions, along with 1,146 working drawings and photographic illustrations. Formerly titled *Cassell's Wood Carving*. 576pp. 6½ x 9¼.
                                                                  23489-4 Pa. $7.95

THE PRINCIPLES AND PRACTICE OF HAND OR SIMPLE TURNING, John Jacob Holtzapffel. Full coverage of basic lathe techniques—history and development, special apparatus, softwood turning, hardwood turning, metal turning. Many projects—billiard ball, works formed within a sphere, egg cups, ash trays, vases, jardiniers, others—included. 1881 edition. 800 illustrations. 592pp. 6⅛ x 9¼.   23365-0 Clothbd. $15.00

THE JOY OF HANDWEAVING, Osma Tod. Only book you need for hand weaving. Fundamentals, threads, weaves, plus numerous projects for small board-loom, two-harness, tapestry, laid-in, four-harness weaving and more. Over 160 illustrations. 2nd revised edition. 352pp. 6½ x 9¼.
                                                                  23458-4 Pa. $5.00

THE BOOK OF WOOD CARVING, Charles Marshall Sayers. Still finest book for beginning student in wood sculpture. Noted teacher, craftsman discusses fundamentals, technique; gives 34 designs, over 34 projects for panels, bookends, mirrors, etc. "Absolutely first-rate"—E. J. Tangerman. 33 photos. 118pp. 7¾ x 10⅝.   23654-4 Pa. $3.00

THE PHILOSOPHY OF HISTORY, Georg W. Hegel. Great classic of Western thought develops concept that history is not chance but a rational process, the evolution of freedom. 457pp. 5⅜ x 8½. 20112-0 Pa. $4.50

LANGUAGE, TRUTH AND LOGIC, Alfred J. Ayer. Famous, clear introduction to Vienna, Cambridge schools of Logical Positivism. Role of philosophy, elimination of metaphysics, nature of analysis, etc. 160pp. 5⅜ x 8½. (Available in U.S. only) 20010-8 Pa. $1.75

A PREFACE TO LOGIC, Morris R. Cohen. Great City College teacher in renowned, easily followed exposition of formal logic, probability, values, logic and world order and similar topics; no previous background needed. 209pp. 5⅜ x 8½. 23517-3 Pa. $3.50

REASON AND NATURE, Morris R. Cohen. Brilliant analysis of reason and its multitudinous ramifications by charismatic teacher. Interdisciplinary, synthesizing work widely praised when it first appeared in 1931. Second (1953) edition. Indexes. 496pp. 5⅜ x 8½. 23633-1 Pa. $6.00

AN ESSAY CONCERNING HUMAN UNDERSTANDING, John Locke. The only complete edition of enormously important classic, with authoritative editorial material by A. C. Fraser. Total of 1176pp. 5⅜ x 8½. 20530-4, 20531-2 Pa., Two-vol. set $14.00

HANDBOOK OF MATHEMATICAL FUNCTIONS WITH FORMULAS, GRAPHS, AND MATHEMATICAL TABLES, edited by Milton Abramowitz and Irene A. Stegun. Vast compendium: 29 sets of tables, some to as high as 20 places. 1,046pp. 8 x 10½. 61272-4 Pa. $12.50

MATHEMATICS FOR THE PHYSICAL SCIENCES, Herbert S. Wilf. Highly acclaimed work offers clear presentations of vector spaces and matrices, orthogonal functions, roots of polynomial equations, conformal mapping, calculus of variations, etc. Knowledge of theory of functions of real and complex variables is assumed. Exercises and solutions. Index. 284pp. 5⅝ x 8¼. 63635-6 Pa. $4.50

THE PRINCIPLE OF RELATIVITY, Albert Einstein et al. Eleven most important original papers on special and general theories. Seven by Einstein, two by Lorentz, one each by Minkowski and Weyl. All translated, unabridged. 216pp. 5⅜ x 8½. 60081-5 Pa. $3.00

THERMODYNAMICS, Enrico Fermi. A classic of modern science. Clear, organized treatment of systems, first and second laws, entropy, thermodynamic potentials, gaseous reactions, dilute solutions, entropy constant. No math beyond calculus required. Problems. 160pp. 5⅜ x 8½. 60361-X Pa. $2.75

ELEMENTARY MECHANICS OF FLUIDS, Hunter Rouse. Classic undergraduate text widely considered to be far better than many later books. Ranges from fluid velocity and acceleration to role of compressibility in fluid motion. Numerous examples, questions, problems. 224 illustrations. 376pp. 5⅝ x 8¼. 63699-2 Pa. $5.00

THE COMPLETE WOODCUTS OF ALBRECHT DURER, edited by Dr. W. Kurth. 346 in all: "Old Testament," "St. Jerome," "Passion," "Life of Virgin," Apocalypse," many others. Introduction by Campbell Dodgson. 285pp. 8½ x 12¼. 21097-9 Pa. $6.95

DRAWINGS OF ALBRECHT DURER, edited by Heinrich Wolfflin. 81 plates show development from youth to full style. Many favorites; many new. Introduction by Alfred Werner. 96pp. 8⅛ x 11. 22352-3 Pa. $4.00

THE HUMAN FIGURE, Albrecht Dürer. Experiments in various techniques—stereometric, progressive proportional, and others. Also life studies that rank among finest ever done. Complete reprinting of *Dresden Sketchbook*. 170 plates. 355pp. 8⅜ x 11¼. 21042-1 Pa. $6.95

OF THE JUST SHAPING OF LETTERS, Albrecht Dürer. Renaissance artist explains design of Roman majuscules by geometry, also Gothic lower and capitals. Grolier Club edition. 43pp. 7⅞ x 10¾ 21306-4 Pa. $2.50

TEN BOOKS ON ARCHITECTURE, Vitruvius. The most important book ever written on architecture. Early Roman aesthetics, technology, classical orders, site selection, all other aspects. Stands behind everything since. Morgan translation. 331pp. 5⅜ x 8½. 20645-9 Pa. $3.75

THE FOUR BOOKS OF ARCHITECTURE, Andrea Palladio. 16th-century classic responsible for Palladian movement and style. Covers classical architectural remains, Renaissance revivals, classical orders, etc. 1738 Ware English edition. Introduction by A. Placzek. 216 plates. 110pp. of text. 9½ x 12¾. 21308-0 Pa. $7.50

HORIZONS, Norman Bel Geddes. Great industrialist stage designer, "father of streamlining," on application of aesthetics to transportation, amusement, architecture, etc. 1932 prophetic account; function, theory, specific projects. 222 illustrations. 312pp. 7⅞ x 10¾. 23514-9 Pa. $6.95

FRANK LLOYD WRIGHT'S FALLINGWATER, Donald Hoffmann. Full, illustrated story of conception and building of Wright's masterwork at Bear Run, Pa. 100 photographs of site, construction, and details of completed structure. 112pp. 9¼ x 10. 23671-4 Pa. $5.00

THE ELEMENTS OF DRAWING, John Ruskin. Timeless classic by great Viltorian; starts with basic ideas, works through more difficult. Many practical exercises. 48 illustrations. Introduction by Lawrence Campbell. 228pp. 5⅜ x 8½. 22730-8 Pa. $2.75

GIST OF ART, John Sloan. Greatest modern American teacher, Art Students League, offers innumerable hints, instructions, guided comments to help you in painting. Not a formal course. 46 illustrations. Introduction by Helen Sloan. 200pp. 5⅜ x 8½. 23435-5 Pa. $3.50

A MAYA GRAMMAR, Alfred M. Tozzer. Practical, useful English-language grammar by the Harvard anthropologist who was one of the three greatest American scholars in the area of Maya culture. Phonetics, grammatical processes, syntax, more. 301pp. 5⅜ x 8½. 23465-7 Pa. $4.00

THE JOURNAL OF HENRY D. THOREAU, edited by Bradford Torrey, F. H. Allen. Complete reprinting of 14 volumes, 1837-61, over two million words; the sourcebooks for *Walden*, etc. Definitive. All original sketches, plus 75 photographs. Introduction by Walter Harding. Total of 1804pp. 8½ x 12¼. 20312-3, 20313-1 Clothbd., Two-vol. set $50.00

CLASSIC GHOST STORIES, Charles Dickens and others. 18 wonderful stories you've wanted to reread: "The Monkey's Paw," "The House and the Brain," "The Upper Berth," "The Signalman," "Dracula's Guest," "The Tapestried Chamber," etc. Dickens, Scott, Mary Shelley, Stoker, etc. 330pp. 5⅜ x 8½. 20735-8 Pa. $3.50

SEVEN SCIENCE FICTION NOVELS, H. G. Wells. Full novels. *First Men in the Moon, Island of Dr. Moreau, War of the Worlds, Food of the Gods, Invisible Man, Time Machine, In the Days of the Comet.* A basic science-fiction library. 1015pp. 5⅜ x 8½. (Available in U.S. only) 20264-X Clothbd. $8.95

ARMADALE, Wilkie Collins. Third great mystery novel by the author of *The Woman in White* and *The Moonstone.* Ingeniously plotted narrative shows an exceptional command of character, incident and mood. Original magazine version with 40 illustrations. 597pp. 5⅜ x 8½. 23429-0 Pa. $5.00

MASTERS OF MYSTERY, H. Douglas Thomson. The first book in English (1931) devoted to history and aesthetics of detective story. Poe, Doyle, LeFanu, Dickens, many others, up to 1930. New introduction and notes by E. F. Bleiler. 288pp. 5⅜ x 8½. (Available in U.S. only) 23606-4 Pa. $4.00

FLATLAND, E. A. Abbott. Science-fiction classic explores life of 2-D being in 3-D world. Read also as introduction to thought about hyperspace. Introduction by Banesh Hoffmann. 16 illustrations. 103pp. 5⅜ x 8½. 20001-9 Pa. $1.50

THREE SUPERNATURAL NOVELS OF THE VICTORIAN PERIOD, edited, with an introduction, by E. F. Bleiler. Reprinted complete and unabridged, three great classics of the supernatural: *The Haunted Hotel* by Wilkie Collins, *The Haunted House at Latchford* by Mrs. J. H. Riddell, and *The Lost Stradivarius* by J. Meade Falkner. 325pp. 5⅜ x 8½. 22571-2 Pa. $4.00

AYESHA: THE RETURN OF "SHE," H. Rider Haggard. Virtuoso sequel featuring the great mythic creation, Ayesha, in an adventure that is fully as good as the first book, *She.* Original magazine version, with 47 original illustrations by Maurice Greiffenhagen. 189pp. 6½ x 9¼. 23649-8 Pa. $3.00

THE COMPLETE BOOK OF DOLL MAKING AND COLLECTING, Catherine Christopher. Instructions, patterns for dozens of dolls, from rag doll on up to elaborate, historically accurate figures. Mould faces, sew clothing, make doll houses, etc. Also collecting information. Many illustrations. 288pp. 6 x 9. 22066-4 Pa. $4.00

THE DAGUERREOTYPE IN AMERICA, Beaumont Newhall. Wonderful portraits, 1850's townscapes, landscapes; full text plus 104 photographs. The basic book. Enlarged 1976 edition. 272pp. 8¼ x 11¼.
23322-7 Pa. $6.00

CRAFTSMAN HOMES, Gustav Stickley. 296 architectural drawings, floor plans, and photographs illustrate 40 different kinds of "Mission-style" homes from *The Craftsman* (1901-16), voice of American style of simplicity and organic harmony. Thorough coverage of Craftsman idea in text and picture, now collector's item. 224pp. 8⅛ x 11. 23791-5 Pa. $6.00

PEWTER-WORKING: INSTRUCTIONS AND PROJECTS, Burl N. Osborn. & Gordon O. Wilber. Introduction to pewter-working for amateur craftsman. History and characteristics of pewter; tools, materials, step-by-step instructions. Photos, line drawings, diagrams. Total of 160pp. 7⅞ x 10¾. 23786-9 Pa. $3.50

THE GREAT CHICAGO FIRE, edited by David Lowe. 10 dramatic, eye-witness accounts of the 1871 disaster, including one of the aftermath and rebuilding, plus 70 contemporary photographs and illustrations of the ruins—courthouse, Palmer House, Great Central Depot, etc. Introduction by David Lowe. 87pp. 8¼ x 11. 23771-0 Pa. $4.00

SILHOUETTES: A PICTORIAL ARCHIVE OF VARIED ILLUSTRATIONS, edited by Carol Belanger Grafton. Over 600 silhouettes from the 18th to 20th centuries include profiles and full figures of men and women, children, birds and animals, groups and scenes, nature, ships, an alphabet. Dozens of uses for commercial artists and craftspeople. 144pp. 8⅜ x 11¼.
23781-8 Pa. $4.00

ANIMALS: 1,419 COPYRIGHT-FREE ILLUSTRATIONS OF MAMMALS, BIRDS, FISH, INSECTS, ETC., edited by Jim Harter. Clear wood engravings present, in extremely lifelike poses, over 1,000 species of animals. One of the most extensive copyright-free pictorial sourcebooks of its kind. Captions. Index. 284pp. 9 x 12. 23766-4 Pa. $7.50

INDIAN DESIGNS FROM ANCIENT ECUADOR, Frederick W. Shaffer. 282 original designs by pre-Columbian Indians of Ecuador (500-1500 A.D.). Designs include people, mammals, birds, reptiles, fish, plants, heads, geometric designs. Use as is or alter for advertising, textiles, leathercraft, etc. Introduction. 95pp. 8¾ x 11¼. 23764-8 Pa. $3.50

SZIGETI ON THE VIOLIN, Joseph Szigeti. Genial, loosely structured tour by premier violinist, featuring a pleasant mixture of reminiscences, insights into great music and musicians, innumerable tips for practicing violinists. 385 musical passages. 256pp. 5⅝ x 8¼. 23763-X Pa. $3.50

AMERICAN ANTIQUE FURNITURE, Edgar G. Miller, Jr. The basic coverage of all American furniture before 1840: chapters per item chronologically cover all types of furniture, with more than 2100 photos. Total of 1106pp. 7⅞ x 10¾. 21599-7, 21600-4 Pa., Two-vol. set $17.90

ILLUSTRATED GUIDE TO SHAKER FURNITURE, Robert Meader. Director, Shaker Museum, Old Chatham, presents up-to-date coverage of all furniture and appurtenances, with much on local styles not available elsewhere. 235 photos. 146pp. 9 x 12. 22819-3 Pa. $5.00

ORIENTAL RUGS, ANTIQUE AND MODERN, Walter A. Hawley. Persia, Turkey, Caucasus, Central Asia, China, other traditions. Best general survey of all aspects: styles and periods, manufacture, uses, symbols and their interpretation, and identification. 96 illustrations, 11 in color. 320pp. 6⅛ x 9¼. 22366-3 Pa. $6.00

CHINESE POTTERY AND PORCELAIN, R. L. Hobson. Detailed descriptions and analyses by former Keeper of the Department of Oriental Antiquities and Ethnography at the British Museum. Covers hundreds of pieces from primitive times to 1915. Still the standard text for most periods. 136 plates, 40 in full color. Total of 750pp. 5⅜ x 8½.
23253-0 Pa. $10.00

THE WARES OF THE MING DYNASTY, R. L. Hobson. Foremost scholar examines and illustrates many varieties of Ming (1368-1644). Famous blue and white, polychrome, lesser-known styles and shapes. 117 illustrations, 9 full color, of outstanding pieces. Total of 263pp. 6⅛ x 9¼. (Available in U.S. only) 23652-8 Pa. $6.00

ACKERMANN'S COSTUME PLATES, Rudolph Ackermann. Selection of 96 plates from the *Repository of Arts,* best published source of costume for English fashion during the early 19th century. 12 plates also in color. Captions, glossary and introduction by editor Stella Blum. Total of 120pp. 8⅜ x 11¼. 23690-0 Pa. $4.50